The Hidden Word

The Hidden Word

Your Story in Scripture

MELVYN MATTHEWS

Foreword by Bishop Jim Thompson

Darton, Longman and Todd
London

First published in 1992 by
Darton, Longman and Todd Ltd
89 Lillie Road, London SW6 1UD

© Melvyn Matthews

ISBN 0–232–51999–4

All quotations from the Bible are from the New
Revised Standard Version, copyright © 1989, Division of
Christian Education of the National Council of the
Churches of Christ in the USA.

The poem 'Somerset Coal' by Melvyn Matthews first
appeared in *Logos – The Welsh Theological Review* and
is reprinted with permission.

Cover: design by Sarah John

Phototypeset by Intype, London
Printed and bound in Great Britain at
the University Press, Cambridge

Contents

Foreword

We are blessed that this book has been written as part of the
Lent course for our diocese, but its usefulness and inspiration
should go far beyond Bath and Wells. Melvyn Matthews
tackles one of the most important experiences of the Church's
life – that is our meditation, our prayers with, through, and
in, the Bible. There are many people who are afraid of fundamentalism which makes the Bible a sort of idol – fixed,
finished and infallible. On the other hand they find the critical
path which is for ever digging up the arguments about the
text and missing its deep application to all our lives equally
irritating. We are caught between the hyper critic and the
biblical zealot.

There are few more important things to the faith and
revival of the Church than that we should all become excited
readers of our Bible. Melvyn helps us do this in what for
many people will be new ways. He helps us see that it contains
our story – it is about us and our personality, our souls as
individuals and as humankind. It is about our journey with
God. He does not just give us the theory, but plunges in
himself and finds there the struggles, the grace, the joy in his
own life and so encourages us to experience our journey in a
new way. Perhaps we shall not understand it all, but if we
wait on the word, God can speak to us. We shall see new
meaning in our lives, strengthen our love of Christ and make
a space in our hearts and minds for God. All I can say is . . .
and 'I shall say it only once' – Read it!

†James Bath and Wells

Acknowledgements

I felt when writing it that this book had been in my subconscious for a long time. Setting it down in words felt like giving birth after an overlong pregnancy. I would like to thank all those who have, consciously or unconsciously, acted as midwives in bringing it to the light of day.

First of all thank you to all those whose comments about the Bible have been grist to the mill of my mind – some of you figure in the pages that follow. Arguing with you and thinking about what you have said has been the source of conception. Then I want to thank Alan Ripley and Russell Bowman-Eadic of the Diocese of Bath and Wells Department of Training who heard I was in labour and prompted the birth. I am also very grateful to Professor Phyllida Parsloe as Chairperson of the Governing Body and my colleagues the Sisters of Sion at Ammerdown for giving me space to think and write.

Above all my wife June deserves the highest praise for her constant loyalty to what she has seen in me and for encouraging its birth. Special mention must, however, go to the St Julian's Community in Coolham, Sussex, for the silence and beauty of their house, their encouraging presence and their library which inspires. This book and the Lent course which accompanies it is dedicated to them with gratitude.

MELVYN MATTHEWS
Lent 1992

Somerset Coal

Now we live on the surface
but all around us in our fields
there are holes, shafts which
go down to the deep of our forgetting.

These mines are the scars on the
skin of our lives,
speaking the wounds of the past.
They are places where we mourn something unfound,
pits of exhausted longing,
wheels of promise
now lost or rusting.

Here and there in our gardens
we dig the black dust of
memories just below the surface,
or jar against the shale
of hurts, hard and unforgiven.

Our miners' lamps have gone out,
hang awkward in the snooker room,
or plastic on the walls of our
simulated cottages.

But then, one silent evening, walking,
breathing deep the warmth of summer,
talking comfortably, resting,
we met again the overseer
standing in his garden, fresh from
his shift.

Mysteriously smiling, he said,
no, they were not closed;
the dark way was open.
We should go down, over the edge of fear
and dig deep into the coal, rich still
in the seams.

Prelude

This book is about the Bible and how we read it. Its purpose is to provide the ordinary Christian with some new ways of reading and understanding the Scriptures. These new ways will be neither critical nor fundamentalist, but attempt to find a way which is new and positive. This 'third way' will enable people to read the Bible (or read it again if they have given up) because it will show them that the Bible is their story, that they are part of it and it is part of them. The stories and images the Bible contains are not historical, lying dead in the past, either to be accepted as true or to be examined as corpses; but are alive, belong to all of us and are deeply embedded within us. The Scriptures are 'true' and feed us because they enable us to see ourselves as part of the story of God and God's people. Seeing that enables us to reflect upon our present experience in a new light, in the mirror, as it were, of the scriptural pattern and be able to assess it for what it is. This then brings repentance and new life.

The book is called *The Hidden Word* because in the twentieth century we do not easily see that our lives are part of the great narrative of the Bible. We think our lives are separate entities, like little balloons, blown about by other forces, and nothing very much to do with the lives of those whose stories we read. This book deliberately contradicts that assumption and proposes not only that there are a number of links or comparisons to be made between our lives and the scriptural narrative, but that there is a whole way of being which is both ours *and* that of the people of the Bible. We are not just like them from time to time, rather there is a real and profound continuity between our lives and theirs. In a very real sense they are our ancestors and we are their brothers and sisters. When we discover this continuity and accept and own it we will live life as it is meant to be lived. We will then live, as the philosophers would say, 'authentically'. This authentic way of living could be called 'living the word'. Indeed, this 'living the word' is real life. To use a metaphor from spirituality we could say that we had discovered our true selves. The life we think we live risks being false and dominated by the forces of this world. The life of 'the true self', our capacity to 'live the word', is hidden from us by those forces and we have to have our eyes opened to the possibility that a new, authentic life is there, waiting for us, as it were. Hence the title, *The Hidden Word*.

The book is divided into two sections. The first part is devoted to setting out the basis for this new way of looking at the Bible. The new way is a synthesis of a number of different approaches. One of them is the new literary approach to the Bible. This is combined with recent developments in spirituality, especially the contemporary renaissance of Ignatian spirituality, and a belief in the presence of Jungian archetypes in Scripture. There has been a considerable amount of work done on Jungian archetypes in Scripture in America in recent years which deserves to be much better known by readers on this side of the Atlantic. The archetypes found in the Scriptures are the archetypes which give life.

All of these approaches come together in this book. The Scriptures provide us with the basic images of our journey towards God. These images are present in the Scriptures but are also present within ourselves. The written word is an indicator, a sign of the symbolic life hidden deep within each one of us. Our task is to read the Scriptures in such a way as to allow these hidden, archetypal patterns – The Hidden Word – to come to the surface, be owned and so stay alive within us. This is how the word gives life. This is how we have faith in God.

The first half of the book will look at these different ways of hearing the hidden word in more detail. Then, after a short interlude when we take stock of where we have got to and what some of the implications of this new way of working may be, the second half of the book is devoted to exploring a number of passages or sections of the Bible in the light of the 'ways of seeing' outlined in the first half. There is no mystique about the choice of passages. They are chosen because they interest me and because I think they are important for our common self-understanding in today's world. The concluding chapter then tries to outline some of the implications of reading the Bible in this way for the life of the Church today. In particular I try to show what happens to an understanding of the Bible as 'the inspired word of God' when the Bible is read in the way I suggest.

That is what the book is about.

All this may give the impression that this is a rather intellectual book and that reading the Bible can only be done properly by people who think in a particular way. This is not the case. The main purpose of the book is pastoral rather than intellectual or theological. It tries to provide a framework for reading and understanding the Bible which brings life to the soul. The book attempts to look at the Bible in such a way that its true but hidden meaning can leap out and we will 'hear' it clearly. This 'hearing' is not just a hearing of the mind, it is also a hearing with the heart, with the whole of the self. When it occurs we are genuinely set free, renewed and released to share in God's activity in the world.

So I very much hope that readers will realise that what I am suggesting here comes out of my own pastoral experience as a parish priest and as a university chaplain. Much of my time has been spent listening to students and parishioners who are struggling with their experience and trying to relate it to the Bible and the teaching of the Church. That is good. Doing just that, however painful, is an essential part of what it means to be faithful to God. But in these years of listening to people's struggles my overwhelming impression has been that people have grave problems in relating what they are and what they experience to what they assume the Bible says. This is where the biggest credibility gap occurs. Reflection on this leads me to the conclusion that the gap between experience and the teaching of the Church is as wide as it is because people carry around within them a number of unexamined assumptions or unresolved questions. One of these is their own self-doubt. Their assumption is that they, as people, together with their experience, are not basically very trustworthy or good. It is assumed that the primary fact about human beings is their sinfulness. This is complicated by further unresolved questions about the status of the Bible itself. Is it literally true or is it simply a tissue of imaginings? For most people, somewhere in their minds there is the unresolved polarity that the Bible is either literally true or critically false. These assumptions or unresolved questions, in one version or another, are always present when the Bible is studied and I do not think I have attended any Bible study when one or more of them did not come to the surface. It is not even that people believe them, it is just that for some reason they are always presented and have to be worked through. However, their presence leaves the human person in a wilderness. If the Bible is literally true then the sinful reader does not match it. If it is critically false then it leaves him or her just where they were, without anything to guide or to inspire. This gap between our own poor self-understanding and our unresolved questions about the text is a pastoral situation which cannot be allowed to continue and it is by and large in response to this situation that this book has been written.

It is undoubtedly true that a far less sceptical approach to the historicity of the Scriptures now prevails, and unbridled fundamentalism does meet with opposition, but my feeling is that however much progress has been made on those more intellectual fronts the gap between the Scriptures and our experience as human beings has not yet been bridged. People still see the Bible as somehow part of the past and their personal experience as being quite separate from it. This is the vital gap which must be bridged. When this is done understanding and wholeness flood the soul. Faith in God can then begin and 'living the word' can commence. And so this book is an attempt to show both practically and, in places, theologically, how we and our personal interior histories are only separated from the great biblical narrative by the thin veil of our own fear and the material forces which cloud and distort our lives.

It may now be clear why I have prefaced this book with the poem 'Somerset Coal' which I wrote after a summer evening's walk my wife and I made in the lanes around our house just south of Bath. My hope is that this book will encourage Christians to stop digging around in the soil on the surface for intellectual proof or ideas which will somehow 'help', and instead take the leap of faith, step into God and go down into the rich seams of life which are still open both within the Bible and within the soul.

1

The Hidden Word

Let's begin by asking the question, 'How do people find God?' This question does not usually give easy, clear answers, but it is a basic one. How does God come into our lives?

Most Christians, as they think about what has happened in their lives, will give a series of answers. They will certainly talk about their personal experience of God, either as an active, saving God, redeeming them through Jesus, or as a real presence in their daily living. They might also begin to talk about prayer and worship as the places where this knowledge is celebrated or known more fully. They might go on to talk about people they have known who have exhibited faith and mediated the presence of God to them and to the world. Sometimes these people are quite unknown or they might be people like Mother Teresa or Martin Luther King or Gandhi.

All of this is good and real. Most of us are much more aware than we used to be of our religious experience and of its importance every day. But as the conversation about how we find God continues further pieces of the answer might be uncovered. As we go on some people might begin to talk about how they have discovered a sense of the presence of God through creation. Some of these people might be scientists whose sense of wonder at the mystery of things has been accentuated by their research. There is a welcome shift in the thinking of many scientists away from the old scientific materialism which linked scientific progress with atheism or agnosticism. Others who will give this answer are those who live close to nature and who marvel at the complexity of the cycles of change and renewal that nature exhibits. If the conversation continues we might penetrate further into people's experience of God and some might even begin to talk about their suffering and how God has carried them through it. This sort of answer is quite mature and needs a great deal of inner strength for it to be part of a person's religious awareness, and a great deal of confidence or a secure environment for them to be able to talk about it, but it is there much more often than we realise. The suffering might be physical or emotional, but many people do find God during such times. Again, all of this is good and true

But in my experience of listening to people talking about their knowledge of God and of God's action in their lives I think there will come a point, if the conversation goes on long enough, when people try to relate what they know about God through their experience – by whatever means that knowledge has been acquired – to the traditional 'givens' of their faith, that is, to the Bible, the creeds and the teachings of the Church. They will try to relate what they know to what they have been told. People are not unaware of the problems here, for they know that what they experience or what they have come to think about God as the result of experience does not always fit easily with what they have been given by the past. What the church has told them and what they have found out for themselves are not always the same thing. Nor is this problem peculiar to religious people, but the church is a particular case in point because it carries within it a considerable number of very strong 'givens' which are regarded as quite central. What these are differs from church to church, but no church escapes them, whether they be the traditional doctrines, the credal formulae, the patterns of worship or the traditional structures of authority. Christians talking about their faith do often find it difficult to relate what goes on in their lives to all of these 'givens', to what the Church calls 'the received tradition'.

The one 'given' which is common to all of the churches is, of course, the Bible. It is the relationship of Christian experience to the Bible which is one of the central problems for the churches today. But it is also an area where I have begun to think that a few bridges can now be built. There is an increas-

ing willingness amongst those Christians whose lives have
been shaped by the tradition of the Church to see that Scripture is an essential part of that tradition. Moreover there are
an increasing number of ecumenical Bible study groups whose
members are finding inspiration together in the text they have
held in common for so long. But many obstacles still remain.
We can see just how sharp the difficulties are if we return to
the question we started with and rephrase it by asking, 'Does
the Bible speak to you of God?' This question will attract a
number of quite different answers. Some people will answer
with an unequivocal 'Yes!', while others will shy away and
distance their experience of God from biblical categories.
Whereas the first group are quite clear that the primary and
definitive means of God speaking to us is to be found in
Scripture, such that we have to subject all our experience of
and reasoning about God to a scriptural test, the second
group will say that the Bible is no more than a means of
revelation to them. It tells them about God or at least about
how God has been revealed in the past to particular groups
of people, but it cannot have more than a referential authority
for us today. We should refer to it because it has some obvious
traditional importance, but our own experience is primary.

Let me illustrate these different reactions from my own
experience. I once preached a sermon during which I said
that we should seek to live lives which conformed more truly
to the patterns contained in Scripture. I can still remember
the effect my words had, even now, some years later. After
the service I was confronted by an angry and puzzled parishioner. She wanted to know what all this was about the
Bible. Just what was I proposing? Was I suggesting that we
should go back to the Bible? Surely there was so much in the
Bible which was quite simply outmoded and, indeed, bar-
baric? Hadn't we in this church got past all that? It was an
interesting encounter and one which has repeated itself in
different ways at other times and places in my ministry. The
lady was obviously very alarmed at the prospect of going
back to the Bible. That was where she had come from. Indeed,
that was where many of the parishioners I was privileged to
serve in that church had come from. They were refugees.

They were refugees from an uncritical fundamentalism. The church where I was vicar seemed to offer them an escape from that since – at least on the surface – it espoused a critical approach to the Scriptures. Many of those who came were glad to be free of the shackles of fundamentalism and became very nervous at any suggestion that what they had fled from might come back, even in a different form. This was the sort of church where discussion groups flourished, but Bible study groups were very difficult to establish. A series of evening sermons on Scripture themes was not successful. The sort of thing that was successful was meetings on personal growth or a discussion on disestablishing the Church. The Bible was simply not particularly interesting news.

But this was only one side of the coin. I met the other side very sharply when, in the same church on another occasion, I attempted to preach on one of the controversies which was facing the church at the time. During the sermon I made some apparently liberal remarks and was besieged afterwards by two vociferous students who said that I had simply thrown away the faith. Once again a lively discussion ensued, but these two students were clearly not in full flight from con-servative Christianity. They were looking for something solid and unchanging and were upset that I had, in their view, failed to provide it. They were at the other end of the scale to the alarmed lady. Whereas the students wanted solid biblical ground under their feet the older parishioner positively wanted to be on skis the whole time! When the students said that they wanted solid teaching it was no use explaining that they had been receiving solid teaching all the time. What I and my colleagues were giving them was not the solid teach-ing they were looking for. What they wanted was more of what my alarmed lady was trying to avoid. They wanted something that gave them reassurance in the face of change.

I was only too conscious of my dilemma. If I gave a more so-called 'biblically based' teaching then I would alienate one set of people who were busy escaping from fundamentalism. If I gave a more liberal or critical point of view then I only fell into very bad odour with those who were looking for something more clear and solid in the confusions of the age.

It was certainly a no-win situation. The only solace was that the dilemma was not mine alone. It was that of the Church at large. The situation hardly needs commentary. Christians today, in all of the churches, are faced with the predicament where the fruits of international scholarship and the felt psychological and pastoral needs of individuals appear to point in opposing directions. The theological battles between the liberals and the conservatives are certainly simplified and caricatured by the popular press but there is no doubt that a set of tensions does exist. What I had experienced on the two occasions I have spoken about was clear evidence that none of us, wherever we found ourselves on the spectrum, could escape the problem.

I have recounted these stories because it is precisely this set of tensions, particularly as they affect the way we read the Scriptures, that has triggered my thinking. The encounters I have described show how one priest's ministry in a moderate and thoughtful Anglican parish was dogged by these conflicts. As a result much of my ministry, probably before but certainly since, has been devoted to making some sense of it all and trying to find a way through to surer ground. For I began to feel then, and have felt increasingly since, that the gulf between the two attitudes I encountered is an artificial one. After a while I came to see that both sides of the divide share a common set of assumptions and are not as far away from each other as they appear. They are both views which rely on the centrality of rational enquiry and so are both products of the rational Enlightenment of the eighteenth and early nineteenth centuries. Like all products of the Enlightenment they find it very difficult to take story and symbol and mystery seriously. They are arguing over the same bone while refusing to look over their shoulders at other and more profound ways of understanding things which are readily available to those with imagination and open eyes and hearts.

On the other hand many people will say that it is hardly necessary to go so far. Why invoke the need to live by myth and symbol when common sense will do just as well? Surely many people, even if they know about them, live with these differences quite easily and are more than happy to leave others to resolve them? If they think about it they might wonder how it will all work out, but broadly speaking it does not affect their faith one way or the other. Similarly we should not exaggerate the matter. We are not all students looking for absolutes nor are we all refugees from fundamentalism! Most thinking people do actually take up a variety of middle views, seeing the need for reason but also trying to affirm a faith which is reasonably settled and confident and which has something to say to the confusions of the age in which we live. People sense the claims of both sides of the argument and come to some sort of working compromise.

But in the end this apparently sensible stance is an uncomfortable one and often taken up for negative rather than positive reasons. It is often a stance adopted out of exasperation and the invocation of common sense is a retreat from the need to do some very careful thinking. We cannot stay in a place simply because every other place that we can see is impossible. Those who find themselves at this point may know that they are neither total radicals nor fundamentalists but this does not relieve them of the responsibility of working out exactly where they are and of finding some sort of clear basis for that position. A combination of anti-intellectual suspicion, resignation and demoralisation has affected the popular mind, at least in many parts of the english-speaking world, since the end of the Second World War. We have to recover a sense of the human person as a properly positive, forward looking, open being, who finds the meaning of life by always moving forward into new horizons, behind each of which God lies hidden calling us always forward.

What I am trying to say is that in the end the principal reason why people are reluctant to abandon the claims of either liberalism or fundamentalism is not so much the attractions of common sense but the lack of confidence we have in the inner, symbolic life. We do not trust our inner selves and our natural capacity to live by myth, story and symbol. We do not seem able to believe that we actually do live by powers unknown or allow ourselves to trust that those powers are benign. We still see the inner life as dark and destructive. In this we are actually much more children of the Enlightenment than we think and both the fundamentalist and the liberal, rational scholar are alike at this point. They would both rely upon the rational certainties which our culture values. Although they are apparently opposed in reality they are mirror images of each other. This has been spotted by a number of contemporary commentators. One of them, an english Dominican, says that both liberals and fundamentalists rely upon the same concept of the 'dispassionate witness' in their interpretation of Scripture. He says, '. . . a fundamentalist reading of the text relies upon thoroughly modern presuppositions as to how a text should be read. It is as contemporary as the relativism against which it protests.'[1] He goes on to say that we find the study of Scripture difficult in modern times, '. . . not because the narratives of the Bible are complex but because we are. We have evolved a particular perception of "homogeneous and empty time" to which, anyway, neither novelists like Joyce nor scientists struggling with special theories of relativity grant unqualified assent anymore.'[2]

This has occurred because we have been unwilling to abandon a way of looking at the world which is governed by the particularity of time and place bequeathed to us by Locke and Newton and those who have followed them. When we read the Scriptures something much more is required of us which our modernity does not allow us to adopt. We have to learn to trust the depths of ourselves and to reckon that those depths are actually in serious continuity with the realities of the stories we are reading. The Dominican writer I quoted above makes the same point when he says,

> Study of scripture invites us not only to enter a different narrative tradition but offers a deep critique of our way of looking at the world. It invites us to surrender the safe security of the disengaged reader, to lose our mastery, to

[1]Timothy Radcliffe, 'Time and Telling: How to read biblical stories', *New Blackfriars* (March 1991), p. 131.
[2]Ibid., p. 138.

give up being 'little mortal Absolutes', to entrust ourselves
to the flow and thrust of a story beyond our control . . .[3]

And, I would add, to trust that the story beyond our control
is, in the end, our own story as well and so, perhaps, more
familiar than we would like.

The truth is that there is, as it were, a hidden cable between
our personal search for faith and meaningfulness and our
search for meaning in the Bible. We think there probably is
a link but most of the time we cannot see it. There are times
when the link between the two becomes very clear but at
others it is, apparently, non-existent. At times we may feel
that certain passages of Scripture light up vast areas of our
life as never before and we rejoice in that, but at other times
this link disappears and there is no clear relationship between
who or what I am and what it says in the Bible. We do
sometimes come to the point of wanting the link between
ourselves and the world of Scripture to be made explicit, but
most of the time the 'disengaged ego' which we have inherited
from the past prevents us from plunging in and making the
link. We are happier to call the study of Scripture 'difficult'.

There is further support for seeing things this way in the
writing of Alastair MacIntyre. MacIntyre is a philosopher
who once wrote about Marxism, but who, in latter years, has
become a Catholic and a very influential and thoughtful
writer. He comes to this point from the study of the history
of ideas, and says that socialism and capitalism are but the
mirror images of each other, both equally products of the
spirit of the age. MacIntyre urges that we look beyond these
polarities and search for a different community of virtue. He
provides a vital insight when he says that human beings are
constituted by their story. He says,

> . . . man is . . . essentially a story-telling animal . . . I can
> only answer the question "What am I to do?" if I can
> answer the prior question: "Of what story or stories do I
> find myself a part?" . . . Deprive children of stories and you
> leave them unscripted, anxious stutterers in their actions

[3]Ibid., p. 139.

as in their words. Hence there is no way to give us an understanding of any society, including our own, except through the stock of stories which constitute its initial dramatic resources. Mythology, in its original sense, is at the heart of things.[4]

When I came across it some years ago this thinking moved the wheels of my mind in a very powerful way. Perhaps, I wondered, the same applied in biblical criticism and we should look for a new way of seeing things, a new community of story, a common way of being with a common mythology, a common understanding which would unite us all, Catholic and Evangelical, liberal and conservative alike. The Bible as our common story would be at the root of this new commonality.

We are aware in our more complete moments that there is some link between our inner, personal meaning and the meaning of what has been given to us by the past. Contemporary novelists work from this assumption all of the time. In theological terms, if we live at the level of our deepest longings then we will come to know that the God of our experiences and the God of the Bible is the one and the same. The reason we cannot link the two easily is not because they are separate in fact but because we are disunited creatures. We are not living from the deepest levels of our selves. We are living with our surface consciousness alone, with reason or sensation only. Once we begin to live at a deeper level of consciousness than the merely rational or sensational and allow ourselves to live from the depths of our truest nature then the two quests will merge into one and the differences will be known to be futile. The cause of our difficulty has not been in the traditions we handle but in the nature of our daily living and our inability to live at a level where reason and experience are united. Because we are not united then the two quests appear to be different and separate. In other words we have lived so long with a divided self that we have projected that division out of ourselves into the way we lead our lives, into

[4]Alastair MacIntyre, *After Virtue* (Duckworth 1981), p. 201.

the way we read our Bibles, into the way we think about God
and into the way we pray.

This much becomes clear, I believe, to anybody who takes
prayer seriously. It is in prayer that the person becomes
united. True prayer is that which emerges from the depths
of our longing for God, which emerges from that level of our
being where all dislocation ceases and we speak as a unity
longing for the source of its life. When we pray in that way
then we begin to realise that what Scripture has to say is not
so very far away from what we want to say. This is an
important realisation for it is the beginning of a healing in
the soul. The point at which it begins to happen is when the
praying person is content with the psalms. Contentment with
the psalms is that point of wisdom at which the person realises
that what the Bible has to say and what he has to experience
are not so very far apart. This point comes when we utter
Psalm 63:

> O God, you are my God, I seek you,
> my soul thirsts for you;
> my flesh faints for you,
> as in a dry and weary land where there is no water.

Or Psalm 62:

> For God alone my soul waits in silence;
> from him comes my salvation.
> He alone is my rock and my salvation,
> my fortress; I shall never be shaken.

Using words like these regularly enables us to see how the
two searches are not two but one. And once we have found
this way in to unitive experience then we shall begin to find
more. We shall see the basic underlying unity of the Bible,
its common flow of images, its recurring patterns and themes.
We shall see the place, for example, that water and storm
play in both the Hebrew Scriptures and the New Testament.
We shall see the patterns of deliverance and the images the
writers use to convey the action of God. We shall see more
than we saw before because our eye is now single and whole.

Once we have seen that there is a continuity between the

psalms and our own needs in prayer then we shall, all being
well, move on to discerning a continuity between our life
stories and the narrative of Scripture. We shall see that the
movement of the people of Israel out of Egypt is not just a
historical event but something which is going on within each
one of us as we move out of our captivity and our Egypt. As
we follow the lives of the patriarchs we shall see how they
provide us with encouragement and basic patterns of engage-
ment with God as we move through our lives.

Nor is this anything really very new. It is something which
was known to the Fathers of the Church. There is an interesting passage in the prologue of *The Life of Moses* by Gregory
of Nyssa, where he defends himself against the criticism that
he is trying, by writing such a treatise, to turn people into
biblical characters. Gregory was writing at the end of the
fourth century in a world of educated aristocrats and intellectuals, trained in the traditions of syncretic Hellenism. He
had the task of demonstrating to Greek intellectuals that the
religion of Christians, with its source in what would have
been considered the barbarism of the Hebrew Scriptures, was,
nonetheless, a religion which would lead to the perfection
spoken of in Greek philosophy. He begins by defining perfection in moral terms, as concerned with 'goodness', and then
advises his readers to make use of the Scriptures 'as a counsel-
lor in this matter'. It is at this point that he has to defend
himself against the accusation that he is trying to make his
intellectual readers into rough, primitive, biblical characters.
He says,

> What then? Someone will say, "How shall I imitate them,
> since I am not a Chaldean as I remember Abraham was,
> nor was I nourished by the daughter of the Egyptian as
> scripture teaches about Moses, and in general I do not
> have in these matters anything in my life corresponding to
> anyone of the ancients? . . ." To him we reply that we do
> not consider being a Chaldean a virtue or a vice, nor is
> anyone exiled from the life of virtue by living in Egypt or
> spending his life in Babylon . . . *We need some subtlety of*
> *understanding . . . to discern how, by removing ourselves from such*

Chaldeans and Egyptians and by escaping from such a Babylonian captivity, we shall embark upon the blessed life.[5]

In other words Gregory sees the Scriptures as being full of what we would now call 'types', patterns for the life of perfection. We are not to become Moses or live like Moses, but we are to see in the movement of Moses' life the pattern of perfection which all of us can follow. Goodness is not just a matter of doing good deeds but of following a pattern of being which brings you into the closest friendship with God. This pattern is given us in Moses' life and the movement of the people of Israel out of Egypt. Gregory believes the Scriptures have a 'spiritual sense', a hidden meaning, in that they provide us with the pattern which is true for all people. What happened to Moses is what will happen to us when we follow the way of perfection. At the end of the book Gregory says to his reader,

Since the goal of the virtuous way of life was the very thing we have been seeking, and this goal has been found in what we have said, it is time for you, noble friend, to look to that example and, *by transferring to your own life what is contemplated through spiritual interpretation of the things spoken literally*, to be known by God and to become his friend.[6]

We face a similar problem. We have to make the Scriptures real for the cultured despisers of our day. This will be done by enabling them to enter into its 'spiritual sense'. In reading the Scriptures we are not being asked to adopt, literally, the ways of Abraham or Moses, but to rediscover for ourselves the archetypal patterns of life which they followed and which if followed by us will bring us into friendship with God. God is not attained, Gregory says, by simply doing good deeds or avoiding evil ones, but rather by moving out of a life of captivity in Egypt. We come to friendship with God by following the patterns of existence hidden in the story of Moses' life.

[5]Gregory of Nyssa, *The Life of Moses* (Classics of Western Spirituality 1978), p. 33 (my italics).
[6]Ibid., p. 137 (my italics).

So there is a direct, but of course by no means exact, correspondence between the 'spiritual sense' of Scripture that Gregory speaks of in *The Life of Moses* and the 'third way' of reading Scripture proposed in these pages. I have been suggesting that we need a new 'third way' of reading the Scriptures which will renew in us the sense that the Scriptures can lead us into a friendship with God. This 'third way' involves accepting that human beings live by powers unknown, by what I have called 'myth, story and symbol' and that once we accept and own that fact then our spiritual progress can begin. Neither of the two principal ways of reading the Scripture with which we are familiar easily take this into account because they are both in captivity to the 'disengaged ego' bequeathed to us by Locke and Newton. We have to re-establish our links with the interior life of myth, story and symbol. But unlike many of those who would agree with this analysis so far, for example many of those in the 'New Age' movements who want to drop the shackles of reason, at this point I have become very clear that there is a direct link between our interior life of myth and symbol and the great narrative of the Scriptures. Our interior life has the shape of a story and we need to reconnect ourselves to that story. We have to be reconnected with the original mythology which makes us whole. This original story is, for Christians, as for Jews and to a large extent for Moslems, found in the Hebrew Scriptures. I realise that such a statement does raise the question of the 'uniqueness' of the Christian way in a particularly sharp form. If you ask why the Hebrew Scriptures and not the Buddhist or Hindu or any other Scriptures then a long discussion has to ensue. My initial point is that we have to accept that we are simply given our original story and have to accept a degree of arbitrariness or 'givenness' about how that came about for us. I want to return to this question at a later point. At the moment I am concerned to set out something of how it all works out in the human psyche.

One of the primary openings – if not the primary opening – into this 'original mythology', this original story which we have been given, is the opening of prayer. The psalms are the basic and communal 'way in'. But once this opening has been found then the rest can follow and we will join the people of God on their way out of captivity and back into the presence and the friendship of God which was enjoyed at the beginning of things when Adam and Eve spoke with God in the garden in the cool of the evening.

This 'third-way' then is to look at the Scriptures as concealing 'the hidden word'. The word is God's way of being for God's would-be friends. What God has been telling us from the beginning is how to be with God, how to remain in God's presence and not perish. This word has been hidden from us because our eyes have been fixed on illusions. Our sight has been clouded because we are living according to our false selves. We have not been living from the centre of our beings but on the surface of things. We have thought that we could attain God's presence by other means, refusing to recognise that God was already present to us. And so we did not hear the word of friendship which he has been uttering for us and to us from the beginning.

Our preoccupations with the mere analysis of Scripture on the one hand, and its literal truth on the other together with all the conflicts which arise from such a polarity have prevented us from hearing what the word has to say to us. The word has been present, 'stored up for us from the foundations of the world', living behind all of these confusions and waiting for us to let them go and 'come to our selves'. When we do that the scales fall away and we can see. It is as if this hidden word has always been there waiting for us to hear it, waiting to rise out of the depths of our being, give us back our true meaning and restore us to our original condition.

2

Stepping into God

In order to hear the word which has been hidden within us from the foundation of the world but which is hidden from us by our own attachment to this world, we have first of all to step out of ourselves and into God. We will not hear what it is that the Bible has to say to us unless we have first made this interior move.

Spiritual people are not those who see a spiritual as opposed to a materialist meaning in things but rather those who live the whole of their lives, including the material parts of them, spiritually. They are those who live with all of themselves as being open to God. This means living from the inner spirit, with the hidden part of ourselves. It means living as those who have uncovered the hidden part of ourselves to ourselves and who know ourselves to be entire and whole before God. This is the religious life – openness to God from the very depths of oneself and an acknowledgement that all that one does is done in God and to God. The religious life is life lived with a personal interior discipline of awareness and attention. Once we live in this way then we will be set free as human beings by God.

In that interior freedom a number of things happen. One is a greater freedom to stand with the poor and the oppressed. Another is a greater freedom from the principalities and powers of this world. Above all we will be free to read the Bible as the story of those who have set out on this interior journey and gone before us on the way. We will find ourselves reading the Bible as the book of the stories of those who have also 'stepped out'. But we will only be free enough to see it

as such when we have taken the risk ourselves and stepped
out into God. What does this 'stepping out' involve?

Something of what this means is to be found in one of my
favourite poems by W. H. Auden. The poem is called 'Atlantis' and it was written in 1941 soon after Auden's conversion
to Christianity. In it he talks about the journey we have to
make to the lost and unknown land of Atlantis, the place of
our desire. The burden of the poem is the need to step out
on the journey towards Atlantis if you are to know anything
about life and its meaning, however foolish such a stepping
out may seem. Those who have persuaded themselves that
there is no such place are likened to the 'witty scholars' of
Ionia.

> . . . but notice
> How their subtlety betrays
> A simple enormous grief . . .

for they have forgotten that to step out on the journey is to
realise the true end of humanity. But the further point that
the poem celebrates is that the journey to Atlantis is under-
taken in and through everything that we experience. Our
journey to Atlantis is not a separate journey, quite different
from our normal, secular journey through life; but a journey
through life at a different level. It is a journey with everything
but one which also leaves everything behind. Indeed, it is a
journey beyond everything but one which cannot do without
everything in order for the journey to take place at all. The
point is being made that those who try to make the journey
with great earnestness, taking the 'spiritual path' with obsess-
ive seriousness, as if it were necessary to be entirely different
from the rest of the human race, will be those who will never
complete it. We are advised, perhaps with tongue in cheek,

> Strip off your clothes and dance, for
> Unless you are capable
> Of forgetting completely
> About Atlantis, you will
> Never finish your journey.

The poem is, like much in Auden, both deeply religious

and a poetic conceit. It is a conceit which hides a truth. This truth is twofold. Above all else we need to step out into the reality of God, but we also need to remember that the reality of God is not a pious construct separate from and negative towards this material reality which we know. The reality of God is not a 'spiritual' reality only discovered by so-called 'spiritual' means. This would reduce God to the level of any other reality. God is actually *the* reality who is present within and includes yet transcends the realities within which we live. God is other than us but is always present to us, hidden within the commitments which we make in this life, an ever present reality which reality celebrates but cannot exhaust.

Behind this insight of Auden's there lies, of course, a theology of 'presence', a sacramental view of the reality of this world. But the particular way in which Auden expresses it has some links with the mystical tradition in western Christianity. In particular it relates to the work of Meister Eckhardt, the German mystic of the fourteenth century. As is now increasingly well known, Eckhardt spoke of God as 'the ground of our being', and of how God was 'birthed' in the soul. For him God was in all things and all things are the way to God. He said, speaking of the contemporary obsession with spiritual experiences, 'Whoever is seeking God by ways is finding ways and losing God, who in ways is hidden.'[1] He speaks of images of God which obscure awareness of God, saying, 'The smallest creaturely image that ever forms in you is as great as God is great because it comes between you and the whole of God . . .'[2] And so what we have to do is to step out of ourselves, out of our creatureliness and let God be God in us. 'Go out of yourself and let God be God in you'.[3] This 'going out' or 'stepping out' as I have called it is itself the work of God and is the birth of God in the soul.

Eckhardt found himself in trouble during his lifetime because of his language, but in our own age we have warmed

[1]Meister Eckhardt, *Essential Sermons* (Classics of Western Spirituality 1981), p. 183.
[2]Ibid., p. 184.
[3]Ibid.

to him, partly perhaps because we are more sensitive to the language of interiority. We are more aware of the psychological journey we undertake. We are now beginning to be aware that without the inner journey the outer journey becomes dominated by what we can only call 'political concerns', just as it is also true that the inner journey on its own, without allowing that journey to spill over into our lives, becomes a pious fiction. But we have been dominated in western Christianity for so long by the 'social' gospel and the need to act and to change things that people are keenly aware of the need for interior refreshment at the deepest level. We need to reassert the fact that spiritual health comes from a 'stepping out', an openness to the presence of God in all things and an opening of the doors of the soul to that reality. Once we begin to talk to people about God in this way then the results are staggering. People turn and listen, they see things new. In fact this way of talking about God opens the human psyche to a deep and entrenched longing for the divine which exists at a very fundamental level within the self but which has been locked away by the forces which control this age. Once we 'step out' and allow God to be God in us or, in Auden's phrase, take 'the Ship of Fools', then instead of the unreason or darkness which we fear, we will find deep levels of strength and light which we will realise we have been denying ourselves for years.

Modern men and women have not totally abandoned themselves to the gods of nihilism. The evidence of opinion polls continues to show that people call themselves Christian even when church attendance is also in very steep decline. The evidence of the same polls shows that people still pray and believe in God even though they do not practise this religion in any formal way. People listen to popular religious broadcasters and attend retreat centres in ever increasing numbers but do not want to give formal allegiance to any of the mainstream institutional churches. However rational or secular we want to be it seems that we cannot rid ourselves of those rumours of angels which continue to buzz around in our heads. So in spite of being apparently one of the most rational and secularised nations in the world we are also amongst the most obstinate in giving up our religion.

People have within them a natural yearning. They recognise, somehow, that they could be religious if only the church or their religious teachers would give them the means to be so. The fact that people say they are religious but do not go to church is not an indication of how they need to be evangelised all over again, but rather an indication that they feel they are naturally religious but cannot find a satisfactory way of being so. They feel that they are in the wilderness without a pillar of cloud by day or fire by night. They want to be religious but cannot, in this situation, find out how that can be done. All of the given alternatives seem to be without coherence, but they wish they weren't.

This should be seen as enormously encouraging, hopeful and positive. Human beings are more people on a journey without maps than people who cannot set out at all. And because of their social and intellectual history they are people who have unwittingly deprived themselves of the tools to build maps. Now we have to look into the real springs of life. When we do this we shall see that once the surface reality of western living is removed human behaviour springs from a far deeper and richer source. We will not open up the human psyche to unreason and dark forces but uncover a deep and entrenched longing for the divine which resides in human beings at a very fundamental level. We will reach into deep levels of light and strength which the attempt to exercise reason has in fact disguised.

This is what we have to 'step into'. Once we do that then we will bring about within ourselves an immense expansion of our religious awareness. To be personal for a moment it is worth recounting that once circumstances allowed this to happen within me I found that I was able to return to my earlier love of literature and the stories and symbols that literature carries and relate them to my faith. The quest for the transcendent in art and music became more important to me. I went on retreat and discovered Thomas Merton who seemed to have followed a similar path and then gone on into a deep relationship with other faiths. Once again this resonated with parts of my life's experience which were lying about like dead bones in my consciousness. It brought them to life and I fell in love with his writings. At the same time I picked up a copy of Thomas Traherne's *Centuries*, which had been a gift to me by a retired Professor in his beautiful house high above the Rift Valley in Kenya and which had lain neglected on my shelves for years, and read his celebration of creation with uncontrollable joy. I found kindred spirits all over the place, but above all I found a kindred spirit within myself. I stopped fearing the supposedly dark irrational forces within myself and found, hidden in the depths, a capacity to love, to pray and to praise which had, in some ways, been obscured by so much else which I had thought important.

Once you descend into the human psyche, once you take away the surface covering of reason and reasonable behaviour, you do not discover total chaos or nothing other than the dark forces of passion and violence. You actually discover a great deal of strength and light. You find much warmth, a deep desire for goodness and love, and an over-whelming ability to give love, often frustrated by the require-ments of reason. I came to the conclusion that it is not so much reason which prevents violence from breaking out but the cult of the supremacy of reason which encourages violence because it exercises a controlling power over the desire for goodness. Indeed there is some evidence to support the view that violence is a disease not so much of those societies which are without reason but of those which have invested too much in reason. Be that as it may, the point is that once I had allowed myself to think the impossible and see that the lack of attachment by human beings to the power of reason was not so much a loss as the gateway into a richer and more positive view of the inner being, then I began to see a way forward. This was a way forward in a number of different, but related directions. It was a way forward in my under-standing of the spiritual life and of prayer – for now I realised that the spiritual life is no more, nor any less, than life lived at great depth, indeed at such a depth that the transcendent presence of God becomes a real presence within the soul. I realised that prayer is not so much the expression of empty

longings in the face of the absence of God but a conversation
with and within the reality of the Father, Son and Holy
Ghost.

It was also a way forward in my understanding of how to
read the Scriptures, for the Scriptures are essentially about
that inner world of light and life which surges to the surface
once the carapace of reason is lifted, or at least the carapace
of humanity's trust in reason is lifted. I have now come to
see that if we are to be set free to read the Bible properly and
in depth then the first thing we have to do is to put the
rational back into its normal place in our scheme of things.
The person who, for me, begins this process best is Fr William
Shannon. Fr Shannon is the editor of the many letters that
Thomas Merton wrote during his lifetime and has been much
influenced by the thinking of that great monk. In his book
Seeking the Face of God Shannon presents us with a way of
praying which is inspired by the work of Merton but also
relates to the teachings of many of the Church fathers on
prayer. In particular he develops for modern Christians the
idea of the spiritual ladder as it is expressed by the Carthusian
monk Guigo II who died in 1188. In his treatise on prayer
called *The Ladder of Monks*, Guigo says that there are four
rungs on the ladder by which we are lifted up to heaven.
Nowadays we do not find the image of the ladder so helpful
as the image of the journey and it is the journey image which
I have chosen, like so many others in the twentieth century,
to use in this book. But essentially they are saying the same
thing for they are both images for the same reality, the movement of the person towards God. In Guigo's work the first
rung of the ladder is *reading*, what he calls 'a careful study of
the Scriptures, in which the person's whole attention is
engaged'. In other words the reading of the Scriptures cannot
be reduced to being no more than a preparation for greater
intellectual understanding of God's ways or the teachings of
the Church. It might well involve such things, but above all
reading the Scriptures, what he calls 'lectio divina', is one of
the rungs of the ladder of spiritual progress. It is part of the
movement of the soul towards God, part of what I have called
'stepping out', or what Eckhardt calls 'letting God be God'

in you. In other words you cannot separate out the reading of the Scriptures from the spiritual journey as if it were an intellectual discipline in its own right quite separate from the spiritual journey of prayer and meditation. It is one of the rungs of the ladder. Fr Shannon says,

> In an age wherein books are available in large numbers, it is important to understand how *lectio divina* differs from simple *lectio*. Whereas *lectio* aims at answering questions and satisfying the curiosity of the mind, *lectio divina* aims more at challenging the heart. While it would be wrong to think of *lectio divina* as anti-intellectual, it would be equally incorrect to think that its purpose is simply to communicate knowledge or information . . . the final goal of *lectio divina* is to initiate and deepen the conversation process in the one who reads. It seeks to draw the reader ever more fully into union with Christ Jesus, who is the perfect image of God. [4]

Fr Shannon's implication is, of course, that in the modern age when we talk about reading the Scriptures we normally mean *lectio* rather than *lectio divina*. It is very difficult for us to see that what is primary is the journey or the ascent of the ladder and that reading the Scriptures is one rung or step upon that process. Fr Shannon goes on to make some very interesting proposals about how we may recover a way of reading of the Scriptures which is actually more like *lectio divina* than *lectio*. He describes the Bible group to which he belongs and how the Scripture passage is read aloud in the group twice in addition to a third, private reading by each individual present. Fr Shannon reminds us that in Isaiah the word of God is compared to rain. He says that there is a need to remind ourselves here of long, gentle rain which penetrates well beneath the surface. 'What is important is that, through repeated, continuous, unhurried reading, we allow our whole persons to be saturated, filled to overflowing, with the Word of God . . . We should let the Word of God happen to us.'[5]

[4]William Shannon, *Seeking the Face of God* (Fount 1988), p. 41.
[5]Ibid., p. 42.

In many ways this is similar to the realisation of a contemporary Jewish teacher, Rabbi Jonathan Magonet. In his recent book about the Bible, Rabbi Magonet talks about the way in which he began to want more from the Bible than was available in those liberal rabbinic seminaries which had struggled to come to terms with the scientific study of the Bible. He says,

> The academic rigour of the scientific approach was important because it still seemed possible to reach some objective conclusions about the history of the texts before us. But the results seemed to do little to nourish the soul of a Jewish world still deeply shaken by the horrors of the Shoah (Holocaust). Somehow the Bible had to become again the source of comfort and challenge and religious growth, without sacrificing the seriousness and, indeed, the important results of the scientific approach.[6]

In order to allow this to happen, to allow the rain of the word to penetrate our souls, or, in Jonathan Magonet's words, to let the Bible become again 'a source of comfort and challenge and religious growth', Fr Shannon proposes a number of simple steps. The first is that there should be regular, ideally daily, reading of the Scriptures. Second, our hearts and minds should be prepared, cleared of all unnecessary rubbish. We should then read the text aloud as the monks used to do, we should read it several times, slowly, and then give ourselves time for reflection upon what is said. All this will enable us to hear 'a word of salvation' which we can then carry around with us during the day.

Fr Shannon's method will need adapting to different people in different circumstances, but it makes the essential point that the Bible is intended above all to be a blessing to the hearer or reader. Part of that blessing may well be found in struggling with the scientific analysis of the text, but the blessing will not be received if that is *all* that is done. In addition the word must be received, absorbed, genuinely 'heard' at a deep level within the psyche. In this way its truth

[6]Jonathan Magonet, *A Rabbi's Bible* (SCM Press 1990), p. 2.

and the truth about the hearer become united in a single truth.

Reading the Bible with the depth of attention Fr Shannon asks for is not unreasonable. It will not take us into a higher state of consciousness. It is more concerned with the inner conversion of the soul to God than with religious experiences or higher states of consciousness. There are a number of so-called New Age groups which do want to do just that. Many of these groups not only eliminate reason altogether but also discount the redemptive role of suffering in human affairs. That is a disaster as we shall see when we come to look at some of the biblical passages which deal with loss and suffering later in this book. But it is important to emphasise this. A number of very severe temptations arise at that point in the road where the religious person is left bereft of tradition and unable to make themselves any maps. There is an emptiness in the modern soul which a number of influences will very quickly fill if we are not vigilant. These influences are like the demons in the parable of Jesus about the householder who swept his house clean. These demons arise because we are exposed to an emptiness. We are exposed to an emptiness because we have been used to reason holding sway. Our whole way of being is based upon that presence and its removal will make us very vulnerable. We will find ourselves totally at sea and riding on a real roller-coaster with very little to guide us. The consequences are that people reach out for solace and sustenance to all kinds of occult practices and strange religions, many of which are concerned with the development of personal growth, self-awareness or the apparent stimulation of states of higher consciousness. These are all the religious equivalent of infantile comfort mechanisms when the toy of rationalism is taken away. They demonstrate no more than the depth of the immaturity of the modern world.

God is invisible, but he is not consumed. He is greater than all things. He is beyond and calls us to live face to face with him above all else. In other words once we come to the realisation that God is, and is greater than all talk about him, then we are in the presence of a darkness which can terrify and dismay. This we have to face. We cannot avoid it by

replacing a quest for him with discussion about how to get
to him. This is the real temptation the demons offer. They
feed on the fact that human beings do not like to be alone
before God. They like the way rather than the burning darkness. The dragons offer the comfort of religion rather than
the way of the living God. Often this trust seems like a
darkness but we have to be confident that this darkness is
the darkness of God's loving presence. When God comes near
to us we have nothing by which we can recognise him and
we often mistake that 'nothing' for absence or emptiness. We
have to 'step out' into God. Francis Thompson, the English
poet said, at the end of his mystical poem, 'The Hound of
Heaven',

> Is my gloom, after all,
> Shade of His hand, outstretched caressingly?

In my pastoral experience, particularly as a university
chaplain ministering to people who traditionally have placed
a great deal of emphasis on the central importance of reason,
I have learned that we have to endure a dark night of the
mind far more courageously than we have been able to do so
far. We have something to learn from this death. We are not
being led into the wilderness for nothing and we have to look
around us in a far more positive way. We have to learn how
to trust the darkness into which we have been thrust and
trust that this darkness is the darkness of God's presence and
so is the darkness of love. We have to turn and face the
darkness and step into it. Otherwise we will find ourselves in
the grip of other dragons and be consumed by them. We have
to live in a very different way now. We have to learn how to
live in the wilderness. The Bible, looked at carefully, is the
map of the wilderness into which we will step.

3

Stepping into the Story

Survival in the wilderness depends upon reaching the next
oasis. Oases are watering places in the desert. Here springs
of water flood out of the dry ground and date palms reach
up to the sky. Here the travellers stop, pitch their tents and
take on water and food for the journey. They rest awhile and
in the evenings gather around the camp-fires to eat and tell
stories. Some tell stories about themselves, about where they
have come from and where they might be going. Others tell
stories about those who have gone before, about their ancestors, those who have been travellers long ago. Some sing
songs, ballads of loss and conflict, poems of fear and longing
and desire. Some of the stories are true to history, others are
true in different ways – true to the inner life of the teller and
his friends. Some travellers are voluble, seeking to impress.
Others sit and listen, checking what they hear against the
stories which course through their heart but which cannot be
found on their lips or in any books. And the story-telling goes
on a long time, well into the night. Some fall asleep where
they sit and the fire grows dim. They love to tell and they
love to listen, for the stories themselves are a kind of food on
the way. What one tells is encouragement for another, but
also each one's story is encouragement for the one who tells
it, since it enables the teller to see, perhaps in a new way,
where he or she has come from and how it was that God
spoke to them on the way. The stories are bread on the
journey, revealing to tellers and hearers the pattern of God's
action in the past and giving a promise of sustenance in the
days to come.

The next morning the travellers set out again in different

directions, grateful for the refreshment of body and soul. The body is refreshed by the food but the soul has been refreshed by the stories that were told. This refreshment is not just derived from the fact that these stories were entertaining – that they certainly were – but more deeply from the fact that they spoke about the human condition. Both the tellers and the listeners have heard about themselves in a different way. They saw themselves in the characters they heard about. They saw their present reflected in the past. The struggles of the past became the food of the present. This is the function of all good story-telling. Their patterns provide us with a pattern for our own existence, which then no longer seems quite so meaningless or confused. We can see that there might be order and sense in existence and so we are able to go on in anticipation waiting for God to strike his notes, as it were, in our own life and to force us in our turn to recognise him as present, calling us to love and faithfulness at difficult moments on the way, just as he did before in the stories we heard.

This parable is not just about the travellers of the past or of the Middle East today, but about ourselves in the church now. When the church assembles it is gathering at an oasis on the way. Metaphorically speaking we have dismounted and left our camels at the door. We have come to this tent of meeting for food and refreshment. We open the books and hear the stories of our ancestors. First of all we hear the stories of our very earliest ancestors, the Hebrew patriarchs. We read of their struggles for freedom and their wanderings through the desert. We hear how they were led out of slavery and came to an oasis which they called the Promised Land. We hear about their great leaders, their virtues and their frailties, of what they did in this land, whom they fought to gain possession of it and what happened to them when they lost sight of how to live within its bounds. Then we move on to hear the story of our ancestor Jesus. He was our forerunner, the one who first taught the way and went up to Jerusalem and called us all to follow. He mapped out the path before us and led us to God. Not only do we listen to the stories about him but we are also given the bread and wine of his life just as he gave the bread and wine of his life to his companions on the same journey many years before.

During this meeting we have to imagine that instead of being in a cold and draughty Victorian or medieval church we are in the desert. High above us what looks like a fan vaulted ceiling is in fact the night sky of the Lord. The pillars that soar upwards are the trunks of the palm trees that soar over the oasis. There are even some churches where the ceiling of the chancel or sanctuary is painted with stars as a reminder of where we really are! And the book which we read, the Bible, perceived within this parable of understanding, is not so much a book of instruction as a book of memories, a set of stories about our past which is read within the religious communities which carry it as a source of true self-perception. The stories are read out for the same reason that the stories are told in the oasis in the desert – to enable the hearers to see themselves as they truly are and be restored again to their rightful place in the history of the community of which they are a part. It is a book of remembering, both in the casual sense of bringing the past to mind, but also in the more profound sense of re-membering, of putting things together which had fallen apart. Re-membering means putting ourselves back together with the past to which we belong and from which we have come. It also means putting ourselves together when we have been dis-membered by the dislocations given to us by the spirit of the age in which we live. Hearing these stories and remembering what they say is to be re-membered by God.

How this is so will become clear from looking at the use to which the Jewish and Christian communities put the Bible on the respective occasions of their most important festivals – Passover and Easter. On both occasions the book is read, whether during the Passover Haggadah or during the Paschal ceremonies, as a means of re-establishing the pattern of the present through remembering the pattern of the past. During the Jewish Passover meal the story of the first escape from Egypt is not just retold but re-enacted. The story is not just a story which happened to ancestors in the past. It is told as an event which has happened to those present. The emblems which are eaten – the bitter herbs, the *matzah* – are all emblems of the Passover out of Egypt but also of the Passover of the participants. This came home to me very movingly on one occasion when I attended a demonstration Passover meal where the participants were victims of HIV or AIDS. The rabbi made the connection between the Egypt of the past and the Egypts of suffering which each one of those present knew as a reality. In many ways such ritual story-telling was the only thing which could reach the depths of despair which existed within those who were there. It not only spoke to their condition at a profound level, it also enabled them to see a possible pattern of healing within their situation. They became part of the Exodus as they danced around the Passover table led by the rabbi singing,

> Go down, Moses! Go down to Egypt land!
> Tell ol' Pharoah, let my people go . . . !

It was they who wanted freedom and the Egypt of their bondage was only too real. Retelling the story of the Exodus had enabled them to place themselves again, to refind themselves in God in a way which no other story had been able to do. Moreover for those of them who were lapsed or disaffected Christians it was perhaps only a re-enactment of this Jewish festival which could make the possibility of deliverance by God real. For them the Church had lost its credibility. Christians and Jews need each other at this point where the institutional Church or synagogue has become inaccessible.

In the Christian Passover liturgy – the Paschal ceremonies which are traditionally held on Easter Eve – the same thing happens. The service begins in darkness and in this darkness, with only the lectern lit by two candles, the ancient stories of deliverance are told. The story of the creation is recounted – reminding the hearers of how God breathed life into the darkness of chaos. The story of Noah is told, how Noah and his family, together with the whole of the animal kingdom, is delivered from the chaos of the flood. So too is the story of the Exodus from Egypt and the crossing of the Red Sea. And then from Isaiah we hear,

Ho, everyone who thirsts, come to the waters;
and you that have no money, come, buy and eat![1]

This summons to life is repeated in the readings from Ezekiel
where God promises a new heart and life for dry bones. And
as if prompted by this promise the attention of the assembly
turns to the door of the church where the new fire is struck,
the Paschal candle is lit, brought into the church and the
Exsultet, the traditional Easter hymn of praise, is sung.

The words of this hymn point up, as almost nothing else,
what is happening. This is the night, they say, when of old
you saved our fathers, delivering the people of Israel from
their slavery. This is also the night, the hymn says, when
Jesus Christ defeated death and rose triumphant from the
grave. But, the hymn goes on, this is also the night when all
who believe in him are freed from sin and restored to grace
and holiness.

In other words the stories that have been told are not
simply stories about the past, about the deliverance from
Egypt or the deliverance of Jesus. They are also stories about
ourselves and about our deliverance, our Passover, our restoration. The pattern of God's activity in the past is not finished,
it carries on and incorporates us. The reason we read about
the patterns of the past is not simply to remind ourselves of
what was but to replace ourselves within their framework and
to enable our lives to become part of that same story.

I have become convinced that it is only really within such
a parable of understanding that the Bible can come alive to
us now. We have to see it not so much as a book to be
examined or dissected but as a book to be heard, full of stories
of which we are a part. If we place it within this context then
its force and capacity to delight and speak to us will be
revived. Perhaps I can illustrate this by proposing two related
but very different ways of understanding how Scripture relates
to us and we to it. The first way is to see the Scriptures as
being something like a box of letters which we have found in
our attic. They are rather dusty and very old, some of them

[1]Isaiah 55:1.

crumbling and difficult to read, with strange handwriting and difficult phraseology from a bygone age. When we do manage to decipher them we find that they are just that, history. They are nice history, interesting history but no more than that, a set of love letters from the past. They are written by a forgotten member of the family and are full of details about when such and such fell in love with somebody else, and the family moved to a new home, and what happened to various younger members of the family who were lost at sea or died in the Great War. They are totally fascinating as a family record and even deserve to be published and read but are hardly, we conclude, very much to do with us now. Times have obviously changed and that is that. We don't think or behave like that any more. We have moved on.

The other way of looking at the Scriptures is to see them as a photograph album which, rather than being in the attic collecting dust, is still in use. This album is one of those modern photograph albums where you slip the photographs into pockets on plastic pages and you are always able to add new pages at the back when you need them. In other words this album is always in the process of being completed. More photographs are always being added. The most recent photographs of yourself and your immediate family stand in a direct line with those of the past and you can turn the pages slowly and trace the family likenesses. You might well laugh at the different styles of dress which obtained in days gone by, and you might wonder at the different patterns of life which the forces of the past required, but it is still your family and you will go on filling the album with new life. And you will know that the God who carries your life is essentially the same God as the One who carried the life of your ancestors.

You might say that the difference between these two 'ways of seeing' is not, in one sense, so very great. There is not a great deal of difference between a box of letters and a photograph album in themselves. In that sense you would be right. They both contain information from the past. The difference lies within us. The difference is in the approach to the past and in particular our understanding of the value that literature from and about the past has for us. The first parable shows us looking to the past for information or truth. The second shows us looking to the past for something different, for roots, for a pattern of life, for symbols to live by, for something which seems to be obscured at present, a word which we cannot hear. This does not, by any means, suggest that the truth about the past is unimportant. This second way of looking at text is not fundamentalist. We look at the way they dressed then and know that it is different. We might even trace the history of these differences and account for the changes that have come about in sociological or theological terms. All that is quite legitimate and necessary, for some of the differences are quite fundamental. But the very existence of these differences does not obscure the presence of other, more important, more profound continuities which are of a totally different order. In the light of those continuities we can read the text as a whole and see it as *something to which we belong*, as something living which carries us with it through the dark and the light places in life.

So what I am suggesting is that we should be able to grow out of the impasse of fundamentalism versus liberalism if only we could see Scripture much more as a story or set of stories which make up our common inheritance and to which, in a sense, we belong. This way of looking at things is embodied, first of all, in the liturgies of Judaism and Christianity. It is also, I believe, fundamental to all human communities. All of them have liturgies which tell stories about their past. All of them re-enact these liturgies to give themselves identity in the present. The liturgies and stories of the aborigines of Australia or of the North American Indians or of the tribes of Africa are testimony to that. These stories are not just stories about how the world began but also about how they as a people began and how they came to be who they are since then. A number of those who have spent some time close to the life of disappearing peoples, like, for example, Laurens van der Post, who lived with and wrote so movingly about the bush people of the Kalahari desert, point out how these stories have so often been lost with the advance of our so-called civilisation. They have disappeared beneath the weight of progress in the apparent assumption that human beings could live by the bread of rationalism alone. Nor have those who are the product of westernised ideals been able to replace these stories with any of their own. We are constantly inventing stories but are unable to settle to one as being the one which made and makes us who we are. We are always looking for new stories, new paradigms of explanation for our condition. Nothing satisfies. Our condition is in a state of fracture.

Along with this built-in and unavoidable restlessness, this inability to settle to a story, we also have to contend with one of the unfortunate long-term effects of modern scholarship which undermines, if it does not destroy, our very capacity to carry story and myth within us. This is the overwhelming obsession with discovering 'historical truth'. We are educated to believe that the biblical stories are not 'historically true'. This in itself is demoralising enough and only serves to reinforce the modern myth that truth comes only in one shape or form. That in its turn undermines our confidence in the importance of living by story, myth and symbol; stories, myths and symbols which are 'true', but in a different sense. Furthermore what then happens is that in reaction fundamentalists assert that the stories *are* actually 'true' because they see how contemporary scholarship has used a limited concept of truth and they wish to re-establish the importance of 'truth' in religion. The difficulty is that they too use a concept of truth which is entirely a production of the same rationalism which has undermined the myth bearing qualities of story in the first place. In that sense 'fundamentalism' is just as much a product of the rationalism of the modern age as the liberalism it seeks to attack. Indeed we are now realising that there is quite a lot of evidence to show that biblical fundamentalism is a much more modern phenomenon than its protagonists would admit and that fundamentalist readings of Scripture make use of many modern presuppositions. Fundamentalism is, as one scholar has put it, 'as contemporary as the relativism against which it protests'.[2] In order to extract ourselves from

[2]Timothy Radcliffe OP, *Time and Telling: How to read biblical stories* (New Blackfriars, March 1991).

this downward spiralling argument we need to reach back beyond *both* positions into an understanding of the importance of story which is neither fundamentalist nor purely rationalistic.

Recognising the importance of story is the first step on this road. I remember once having a conversation with a young ordinand whom I had encouraged to enter the priesthood. He came to see me some years later and during the conversation admitted that he now found the whole of the Old Testament completely irrelevant. He couldn't read it any more and was sure that it should not be studied at college, particularly now that it was all so discredited. Nothing in it was true. I was at first silent, because I understood his dilemma but also knew that in some strange way he was quite wrong. Then I knew why. I remembered what someone had told me about the Church in Africa – something I later discovered to be true for myself when I worked in Kenya – that African Christians find the Old Testament much easier to understand than Europeans because they are so much closer to its thought forms and to the history it contains. Its history is their history. They have known the slavery of colonialism. They know of the crossing of the Red Sea into freedom and the Promised Land. They know the difficulties of settling there and the temptations which that land provides once roots and origins are forgotten. The history of the different kings of Judah and Israel is their history. They know they have to remember that once they too were aliens. They can read the Old Testament because it speaks to them about themselves. It remains their history. We find it more difficult but not because it is untrue. We say it is untrue because we have forgotten where we are and have abandoned the quest for common myths and symbols by which we may rediscover our lost identity in the wilderness of rationalism into which we have come. We are looking for truth rather than manna.

The encouraging thing is that over the past few years there have been a number of developments in the way we understand faith and religious belonging and in the way we can read sacred texts. They will help us into a new attitude and enable us to take a step forward out of the impasse of fundamentalism versus liberalism which has so bedevilled the Church of the first half of the twentieth century.

The first of these developments is an understanding of the Bible as literature. Perhaps I can best explain what this approach involves by recounting how I first came across it and what effect it had upon me. I was fairly new to my present work of hosting residential events promoting reconciliation and peace when we held a weekend conference where Jews and Christians looked together at the Hebrew Scriptures. That weekend the passages selected dealt, as it happened, with Abraham and some of the women in the Genesis narratives. We divided into groups and I decided to sit in and listen to the discussion. I was dismayed to find the general approach impossibly literalistic. I was used to the conventional wisdom that Abraham was not so much a person as a cipher for the Hebrew tribes which had moved out of what is now Iraq into Judea. The narrative, I thought, was about the social movement of peoples and not about individuals. It certainly did not tell us anything about Abraham's personality. I was somewhat disturbed that this wisdom was being ignored and that Abraham was being treated as a historical personage with personal attributes. Moreover scant regard was being shown for the documentary hypothesis and the different levels of text within the narrative. Nobody asked whether the section we were reading was from the different levels known to scholars as J, D, E and P and so no one knew whether it carried a particular theology or was determined by a particular historical and social setting. Moreover, nobody seemed to care. When I raised these points in discussion there was little comprehension, or rather, little acceptance of my point of view. I was told that such concerns were not under consideration. What was important was the text as received. This was what our respective traditions, whether Jewish or Christian, had to deal with in the end. I asked about the risk of a textual fundamentalism, but it was clear that there were no fundamentalists here. People wanted to deal with the text as it stood. They recognised well enough that it contained many layers of additions and may well have gone through the hands of a number of different editors before it reached its final form. The different textual strands known as J, E, D and P were accepted but then placed gently but firmly in the background. What was important was what the final editor had intended to convey by allowing the text to take the form that it did. In other words we were back with a piece of literature, a story, which spoke to us and we had to find out why it spoke as it did and to share what it said to us, Jews and Christians alike.

I began to realise that there was far more sophistication in this point of view than I had thought and that my criticisms were ill-placed. I came away slightly bruised but determined to learn more. The truth was I was slightly out of touch. Things had moved on since I had gone through my education and I had not kept up in this area. So I began to read. What had happened was that scholarship had moved on and that some people were talking about the importance of the literary texts within Scripture and asking us to treat them as literature first of all. This approach had the advantage of moving beyond arguments about the truth of the narrative. Is the Genesis narrative, it was asked, made any more meaningful as a piece of literature when we know that it comprises of a number of different 'documents' labelled J, E, D and P and dating from different periods of Israelite history, all put together in one amalgam? Would it not be better to read each book as a whole? Will we not then see parallels with other pieces of literature, even with literature in our own day, and so be able to see more clearly the worth – rather than the origins – of the book as it stands? And will that not happen more easily when we place the texts in a literary rather than a research context? Isn't it better, for example, for us to study the way in which the character of Joseph is portrayed in Genesis and to see the patterns that exist within the story rather than worry about how it was all put together? We will then be able to see how the story-teller brings out the ironies in the narrative and how reconciliation breaks through the enmities between brothers? Isn't it better to see that than to know how the narrative came into being? In the New Testament isn't it better to see how St Mark, for example, uses the imagery of the shore as a place of encounter and discovery

or how St John uses the device of masking the identity of
Jesus (but we the readers know), rather than to surmise which
Gospel was first or speculate on where the Gospel originated
or how many sections are dependent upon one another?
Surely it is better to delight in the books as books and to
enjoy and savour their contents and allow their 'meaning' to
enter our lives in more subtle ways than the scholars seem to
allow? What has happened simply to enjoying reading?

After a while I began to see how reading the Bible like this
brings the books alive in a way which nothing else seems to
be able to do in our generation. It makes them readable again
and lets them speak to our age. In my search to discover
more about all this I came across one essay in particular
which brought it all home. I found this in a book which I
had been given many years ago. The essays it contains outline
some of the different ways of representing reality in European
literature. I had read the book when I was given it and
forgotten all about it. Now my attention was brought to it
again and I took it down. The book is important because the
opening chapter begins by comparing the narratives of the
Hebrew Scriptures with those in Homer. It is a bold and
startling comparison – a comparison of literary forms and
why they are used rather than an examination of literary
origins – but it yields startling results. Both Homer and the
Hebrew Scriptures are concerned with history. Both are of
epic quality. But they differ in their presentation of human
affairs. The author writes,

> Herein lies the reason why the great figures of the Old
> Testament are so much more fully developed, so much
> more distinct as individuals, than are the Homeric
> heroes . . . So little are the Homeric heroes presented as
> developing or having developed, that most of them –
> Nestor, Agamemnon, Achilles – appear to be of an age
> fixed from the very first . . . Time can touch the latter only
> outwardly whereas the stern hand of God is ever upon the
> Old Testament figures; he has not only made them once
> and for all and chosen them, but he continues to work on
> them, bends them and kneads them, and, without destroy-

ing them in essence, produces from them forms which their youth gave no grounds for anticipating.[3]

I found all this very interesting and exciting. It gave me back the Scriptures in a fresh way. I found I was no longer reading with my mind closed to the resonances of the passage concerned, no longer reading with my eye on the circumstances which produced the text. I later discovered that I had become what is now known as a thorough anti-deconstructionist in literary terms, but whatever I was I knew I had, in a sense, come home to a love of literature and found that love just as real in reading the texts of Scripture as I had found it in reading Proust or Balzac when I was a student. I found contrasts and likenesses not only with the writing of Homer, but also with others and saw the Scriptures as standing right at the beginning of a long literary tradition of the representation of reality which has deeply influenced who we are and how we see ourselves and, above all, how we understand the divine in relation to human affairs.

This, however, is where the question comes for so many. Surely, they will say, the Bible is a different sort of book, one which cannot be compared to other books? Surely it not only records unique events but does so in a singular way? Surely it is a holy book which cannot be placed in the same category as everything else? I must admit that this was not something which had occurred to me in the first flush of rediscovery, but once the question was asked I recognised it as being just the question that would worry so many. Large numbers of people will say that considering the Bible as literature undermines its unique quality and the unique value of the message it contains.

But it is precisely this emphasis upon the 'uniqueness' of Scripture which is so questionable. The Bible is hardly unique in that sense. So much of it is simply the literature which the Jewish and Christian communities chose to be Scripture. Certainly that gives it a supremely important status for those

[3]Erich Auerbach, *Mimesis – The Representation of Reality in Western Literature* (Princeton 1953), p. 17.

communities, but any cursory examination of the process by which those choices were made will show that on occasions they were highly arbitrary, sometimes as much to do with familiarity as with value and that much which should have been included was omitted. Certainly some books which did eventually make it into the canon are hardly of the highest calibre. Nor is it a sustainable truth that the books of the Bible were originally written with the intention of bearing a unique message to future generations. They were written to record history, to indicate the value of past events, to try to explain or teach, to entertain or convey religious awareness. They were written for a multiplicity of purposes which cannot be all subsumed into the word 'unique'. The trouble is that our upbringing has encouraged us to read the books of the Bible with an eye to their inner or hidden theological meaning and to elicit from them the bearing, particularly the moral bearing, that this meaning might have on our lives today. We read the books of Scripture so that they can legitimise the evangelical or apostolic commitment which, on other perfectly acceptable grounds, we have devoted ourselves to fulfilling. In other words we have been traduced into reading Scripture through the spectacles of an imaginary preacher looking for the message we can apply to our lives. This has, in a very subtle but sure way, actually undermined what the Scriptures really are in themselves. We will know them better, it seems to me, when we read them with the same critical faculties and the same expectations that we bring to all great works of literature.

With any poem or novel or play which we read or see we come to it anticipating that it might open us up to realms beyond what we know and give us new perspectives on life and on the action of God within those lives. We look for it to bless us. But we also bring along, to that very same reading or that very same performance, intelligence and critical awareness as to how it blesses us and why it fails to bless if such it does. We talk in the interval about the playwright and why and where he or she wrote the play. We talk to our friends about the novel and compare it to others by the same writer or from the same period. None of that is lost. But what we do not do – because it does not have any authenticity and because we know it would be artificial if we did – is read the novel or attend the play as if it were from the outset 'different' or 'unique', or as 'having a meaning for me'. It might well turn out to have 'a meaning for me' and we are glad when it does, but we read the novel or attend the play in open expectancy rather than predetermined orthodoxy. Such an attitude would automatically undermine the original power and quality of the work which we face.

Reading the Bible in this way, as we would read any great literature, does not mean to say that the books it contains do not have meaning; but it does ensure, more assuredly than the traditional church-related approaches, that the meaning which is found is true to what the book actually is in itself. We have to let the books speak for themselves. We have to open the pages and find there what there is to be found in all its freshness, in all its awkwardness and in all its obscurity. We have to struggle with what we are given rather than elicit meanings because we think there must be a meaning which must be in accord with traditional beliefs. If we think there must be a meaning somewhere in the text we will usually read into the text a meaning which is already hidden within ourselves. If the traditional beliefs are true and real then they will surface again and again from an open-handed approach and will be seen to be all the more authentic because they cannot be avoided or lost whoever reads the books at whatever point in time. The books of the Bible clearly contain more meaning than the author or authors intended them to contain. But this is also true of all literature and the sign of great literature is that it continues to hold meaning or significance for people generation after generation. It does not undermine the authority of the Bible to speak of it as literature because every major work of literature speaks with authority. The point is that the authority is not given to the books by tradition but found by the tradition within the books. The Christian community continues to find meaning and divine authority within the New Testament in almost the same way that the community of English speaking people, for example, continues to find meaning within the works of Shakespeare.

While I was struggling with all this I came across a beautifully intelligent and suggestive book which pushed my understanding of the question further than anything else. This was a book by a professor of literature who had turned to the Scriptures, learned Hebrew and ended up working with Jewish scholars, among others, on the meaning of Scripture. The author is Gabriel Josipovici. His book is called *The Book of God*. In it I found something which deserves to be pondered over and over again by protagonists on all sides of the debate about the authority of Scripture. It is a remark which cuts both against those who would effectively reduce the Scriptures to being the sum of historical investigation about them *and* against those who would isolate the Scriptures from the literature of humankind. Josipovici says,

> Our task is to wrestle with this book as Jacob wrestled with the 'man', in pitch blackness, and not for the mere sake of the contest or in order to wrest the book's secret from it, but in order that we may hear it utter its blessing upon us. But that, we must not forget, is what we would expect of our encounter with any great book.[4]

The spirit of that remark was one which has enabled me to turn back to a book which had become exhausted – a mere skeleton which no longer spoke, a bare cupboard which no longer fed me. The long-term effect of the critical method upon me as someone who was bound to expound Scripture week by week to the faithful had been exactly that. Others had said the same. The Bible had become a book upon which we hung our ideas, which served to provide examples to illustrate our prejudices. Now it could begin to live again in its own right.

[4]Gabriel Josipovici, *The Book of God* (Yale University Press 1988), p. 28. (See also his remarks about the uniqueness of the Bible on page 307.)

4

Stepping into the Patterns

It is natural to think of the biblical narrative as the map of the way forward. It is a way of understanding the Scriptures which has great power and attraction. The difficulty is that the biblical narrative is not always a narrative. Every so often it stops and becomes poetry or parable, law or argument – anything rather than story. There are check-points, as it were, when the narrative has to stop moving forwards and look at itself, look around and hold a debate while it thinks about who it is and where it wants to go. It is as if there are bearings to take, demons to cope with or inner conflicts that have to be resolved before the journey can continue.

Sometimes these checks are of the utmost charm and interest, like stopping to sightsee on a long journey. The biblical narrative seems to digress occasionally, turning the corner into curious byways before going on. These byways give the impression of being diversions which are of no real importance and which make no significant contribution to the main plot. Two of them are the little books of Jonah and Ruth, which suddenly appear before the reader like two five-minute sketches which will keep us occupied while the scene-hangers are at work behind the curtain. It is only with hindsight or with the most attentive reading that we realise that they are of immense importance, make a vital comment on the way everything is going and offer a different perspective to the main story, which we miss at our peril.

So every now and again the main narrative has to stop and look at itself, check itself, look around and debate within itself for a while about its identity and credentials, ask a few awkward questions and then move on from where it had stopped. The reader can find this irksome. We want to move on. We have got some idea now that there is a plan or a movement. We have begun to sense that we are going somewhere. We already know something of the plot, what we want to find out is how the writer brings it all to a satisfactory conclusion. But it keeps stopping and telling us things we don't think we want to know, slowing us down so that we are tempted to turn up the ending and read it like impatient people with a detective novel.

The Book of Job is an example. Here, suddenly, in the midst of the great sweep of the Hebrew Scriptures onwards through exile and return, we are presented with a story about a man who loses all of his possessions. And it is plainly a fable, for it begins with God calling together the court of the gods of which Satan is one. It is not history. And our patience is stretched to the very limit not just by the arguments between Job and his so-called comforters, but also at the end, when God presents his case and asks Job if he was there when everything was created. Nothing is really resolved, for who can argue with God when he brings the whole thing to an end?

Now we can, of course, take the scientific point of view and decide that the Book of Job is an old folktale known to other biblical writers (e.g. Ezekiel in 14:12–20), which has been taken up and reworked by a more profound thinker who was a survivor of the Babylonian Exile and its crisis of faith. In other words it is a product of a particular time and set of circumstances which reflects the theological attitudes of those who had been through a certain historical crisis. But although all that would be true it would hardly be enough. For we know, in the end, that the book is talking about us and our own sense of powerlessness and loss in the face of tragedy. It might well have come out of a particular historical crisis of faith, but it becomes 'the classic expression in world literature of the irrepressible yearning for divine order, baffled but never stifled by the disarray of reality'.[1] It is not only timeless but

---

[1] Moshe Greenberg in *The Literary Guide to the Bible*, ed. Alter and Kermode, (Fontana 1987), p. 301.

it is also pertinent to all those who are innocent sufferers. A liberation theologian has seen this and relates the book explicitly to the suffering of the innocent in Latin America. He then relates it to people throughout the world who have suffered and whose suffering we can only look at in the shadow of the Holocaust.[2]

So by stopping for a while with the old fable of 'Job the Patient' the Bible opens up a vast area of reflection which, if we had simply pressed on regardless, waiting for the next adventure, we would have lost and been the poorer for it. The pause helps us. It forces us to think through the tragedies the surrounding narratives have told us about, but then also to reflect upon the purposes of God in unmerited suffering both in the biblical history and so too in the tragedies of which we are a part and from which we suffer. For it is not just a journey onwards which we have to make. It is also a journey inwards, a descent into the unknown of the self. Most of the time we conceive of the journey in linear, progressive terms, as a journey outwards and onwards, a journey over the far horizon towards the promised land of God. What we also have to do is to travel inwards and to deal with the demons within. We have to struggle through to a deep sense of the inward presence of God as well as a sense of the God who beckons to us from the future. This inner journey is, however, often the most feared.

One of my discoveries in pastoral work was that it is very difficult to convince people that who or what they are really matters and that God is to be found in what they are. For so many Christians their personal identity is non-existent or has no value or worth to God. Who they are means very little. What is of worth is what they can do or what they can achieve. Sometimes this mistrust of the self derives from mistaken theological teaching about the value of the self and the nature and location, as it were, of God. But usually these misconceptions are adopted simply because of an interior lack of self-confidence. This lack of confidence is then reinforced by the

---

[2]Gustavo Guttierez, *On Job – God-talk and the Suffering of the Innocent* (Orbis 1987).

immense pressure in our society to achieve or conform to certain exterior role models. It may also derive from patterns of parenting where the parent expects the child to behave in certain ways. I have encountered so many people whose lives have been blighted by the demands of one or both of their parents and where religion has been used to reinforce the authority of the parents over the child, such that in later life the person finds it immensely difficult to believe that they are loved for their own sake and that grace is a free gift. For such people it is always 'other people' who are holy or good, always others who are happy, always others who can do things or meet people or talk easily, attract love, fall in love or become anything worthwhile.

But in more recent years theologians have increasingly been turning to psychology to help them rediscover a sense of personal worth within the individual. In this search they have been greatly helped by the work of Carl Jung. Many people become nervous, not to say frightened, at the mention of psychology. They conjure up within themselves visions of being placed on the psychiatrist's couch and being exposed to the depths of their inner beings. This is frightening not just because of the exposure involved but because the inner being is popularly regarded as being inhabited by darkness – irrationality, dark complexes of various kinds and evil intentions which are only kept under control by the exercise of reason and will-power. The inner sanctum of the human person is often regarded as being a dark place which is best left undisturbed. Carl Jung is the man most responsible for enabling us to see that this view is very limited and shortsighted. He showed us not just that we should not be afraid of our unconscious, but that we actually need to befriend it in order to become whole.

What Jung believed was that the unconscious is at work within us all of the time. We live everything through the unseen lenses of our unconscious selves. Everything that happens to us, everything we see and everybody we meet is filtered and interpreted through these unseen spectacles. These spectacles are formed at a very early stage in our lives and are very much the product of the intense experiences,

both good and bad, of our upbringings. The process might
be compared to the way in which an unseen magnet beneath
a sheet of paper organises the iron filings lying in view on top
of the paper. There are similarly powerful forces at work
within ourselves organising our experiences for us. Initially
this is a threatening realisation, but Jung's view was that
health or wholeness eventually comes when we recognise that
we do have an unconscious and accept and own what is
happening to us. Lack of wholeness, conversely, is the result
of denying these processes. What happens is that we try to
live as if these processes of filtration and interpretation did
not exist and even try to suppress and deny them. It is when
we deny the role of the unconscious that trouble comes to the
soul. Health comes then from a gradual acceptance and
owning of the interior life.

What Jung stressed was that we had to realise that the life
of the unconscious is not automatically dark or bad. It has
within it both light and dark but the dark areas are as important and, potentially, as life giving – if not more so – as the
areas of light. There is a shadow within us but it is the
rejection of the shadow, not its presence, which leads to disaster. Our rejection of the shadow, when it is fierce and strong,
takes the form of projection. We project the shadow out of
ourselves and out onto somebody or something else because
we cannot bear the darkness and the division within ourselves
that the shadow appears to create. But the moment when we
think we have achieved light within us and cleared out the
demons is in fact the most dangerous, for all we have done
is project the demons elsewhere and unwittingly made them
more powerful than ever. Then they will, as in the parable
Jesus told, come back to destroy us with even greater force
than they originally possessed. So the soul is not automatically
a place of darkness which needs to be penetrated by light. It
is only truly dark and bad when *all* that is within it, including
the shadow, is not owned and accepted. Jung's view was that
most people try to deny the unconscious a great deal of the
time. He also came to the view that religion was one of the
main tools or instruments which people used to do this.
Instead of being something which brought salvation religion

was used to avoid the descent into the self which brought health. He said,

> People will do anything no matter how absurd to avoid facing their own psyches. They will practice Indian Yoga and all its exercises, observe a strict regime of diet, learn theosophy by heart, or mechanically repeat mystic texts from the literature of the whole world – all because they cannot get on with themselves and have not the slightest faith that anything useful could ever come out of the psyche.[3]

The interesting and important suggestion which Jung made was when we recognise our tendency towards repression and projection and reverse it to make the difficult inner journey towards integration and wholeness, then a number of things happen and a number of important and health giving discoveries are made. The most important of these is, quite simply, the initial realisation that the unconscious exists and that it is not a threat to our personal well-being. Our real life comes from a deeper level of consciousness than that provided by reason alone. When we do that and allow that deeper level to come to the light of our self-awareness and when we play our part and co-operate with it, then health and wholeness will follow.

An even more important further realisation is that at the unconscious level of our lives we do not entirely belong to ourselves. At that level we belong to one another. There is, Jung came to believe, a collective or universal unconscious where we are all bound together in a greater whole and where we can all discover a greater unity. Here, at the level of what Eckhardt – whom Jung read with great interest – called the ground of our being, we are at one with each other and God. But that was not all. In this collective unconscious Jung came to the view that there are a number of basic patterns, what he called primordial or archetypal images, which are determinative and which we struggle against or repress at our peril.

---

[3]C. G. Jung in *Selections from the Eranos Yearbooks*, on Spiritual Disciplines. Cited by Thomas Merton, *Conjectures* (Sheldon Press 1965), p. 247.

He believed that the world of archetypes was represented in story form in Greek mythology and that these stories were representations of the basic patterns which lie within our collective unconscious. He also believed that whereas there were numerous archetypes two particular ones were of basic importance. One, the shadow, we have already talked about. The other was the basic pattern of masculine and feminine. Male and female need to recognise their need of the other and the presence of the other within them. Once the male accepts the presence of the female within him and owns that presence then he is united with his true self, and vice versa.

This little excursus into the world of Carl Jung is probably familiar territory to many readers for its importance for religion has already been realised by many theologians. In particular its importance for a proper understanding of the processes of redemption has been particularly influential on Christian theology. Looked at through Jung's eyes redemption is the process by which men and women become reconciled to God by acknowledging and owning the shadow which properly belongs to them but which they have projected onto others and so caused conflict and division where there was none. Jesus Christ, seen in this light, is the one who leads the way in both teaching us to refuse to project evil onto others and in embodying that teaching in his own life and death. On the cross he refuses to project blame and absorbs, in a redemptive moment, the shadow into himself. In that process he dies but is liberated into the new creation of the resurrection. We are also beginning to understand prayer more thoroughly and to see its central importance more surely because of the work of this great man. Prayer is the process of opening the self to the wholeness of God and allowing that wholeness to permeate into our lives. It is the portal of the divine within us.

What is perhaps less obvious is how this world of the inner shadow and the collective unconscious, this world of personality types and archetypes, can be of use to the ordinary Christian who wishes to read the Bible. Jung's way of looking at things helped me to rediscover the importance of the Bible when I was struggling to find a way of preaching to the very

articulate and self-conscious suburban congregation which
the reader has already met in an earlier chapter. It was quite
clear that biblical exposition of either the old kind – drawing
dubious moralistic conclusions from the text – or of the new
kind – pointing out how distant this text was from the modern
consciousness – was not adequate. The first because it was
largely unjustified, being more a means of reading in to the
text what the preacher wanted to say anyway; the second
because this distanced the text so far from its hearers that it
ceased to be any means of blessing whatsoever. But most
members of that congregation were sharply aware of psychological categories. Images associated with personal growth
came easily to them. The possibility of archetypes was quite
familiar. And so I began to put together what I knew about
the hidden patterns of the Scriptures with what they knew of
the hidden patterns of human behaviour. In fact we both
knew quite a lot about either side of the equation, but the
essential connection had to be drawn out by the preacher.

The key to all this was to be found in the importance Jung
places upon archetypal or primordial patterns of human self-
understanding. We saw how he claimed that Greek mythology
contains the great archetypal patterns of our collective unconscious. It was but a short step from there to see that the
stories found in the Scriptures could be seen in the same light.
They are the stories which actually form the basic patterns or
archetypes of Jewish and Christian self-understanding. These
patterns are those of 'liberation from Egypt', death and resurrection, feeding on the manna of God and so very many more.
It is by accepting and owning these patterns that we find
faith and life. In owning them the divine enters our lives. It
is within them that we find salvation. They are the basic
images, the basic models for our lives. We have always been
part of these patterns and in so far as we make them our own
we reach the wholeness that God has in store for us. It is
when we fail to read and hear the words of these stories that
we fall away from belonging to the basic pattern of God's
activity and so fall away from our place within God's life.

Perhaps we can now see more easily the importance of the
'pauses' which occur in the Scriptures of which we spoke

earlier. These are the moments when the narrative breaks away from history to reflect upon presence. Biblical theologians have spent a very great deal of time in the past pointing out how the God of the Hebrew Scriptures is a God of history, making himself known in and through the movement of history. All of that is true and important. It is also true and important that God is a presence in and to the human person, a presence which does not depart and which is not dependent upon historical events or only known when we read historical events in a particular way. The pauses in the Scriptures allow us to become familiar with that and encourage us to look beyond the movement of history to the God who is present within ourselves as well as beyond our history. But more than that. These pauses are also portals, gateways into the collective unconscious, openings into the archetypal patterns or symbols which the Scriptures contain. These pauses allow us to step into a deeper world, a world where God's patterning for our human lives is to be found. For deep within the movement of history, deep within what I have called the great biblical narrative, there are also deep-laid patterns, ways of being, archetypal structures which God has placed in existence and by which we must live. We have to re-find these hidden patterns if we are to be healed, we have to own them if we are to come to new life, we have to live by them if we are to become who we are meant to be. These patterns are part of the hidden word of God for us. They are the ancient values which we have, as a civilisation, lost, they are the secrets of God from the foundation of the universe.

Nor are these secrets, these hidden words, esoteric. They are not things for the cognoscenti while the poor are too uneducated or too inexperienced to understand. Just the reverse. They are often things which the poor and unenlightened understand far better than the cognoscenti, for they are so often represented by that word 'values', and very often by 'moral values', or ways of behaving and being, which the so-called enlightened or liberated have learned to scorn. These archetypal patterns of being are not patterns of 'experience'

either. 'Experience' is so often little to do with it. True religion
is not so much a matter of experience as a matter of behaviour.

No, what lies hidden within the Scriptures are patterns of
being through which, once we adopt them, we find new life.
It is as simple as that. Just let us return to the Book of Job
for a moment. Job is asked at the end of the book to place
his trust once again in the mystery and greatness of the
creator God. This is a basic pattern of life which, while it is
not ultimately intellectually satisfying, brings rest and final
contentment to the soul faced with suffering. It is not denied
that Job has the right, indeed the duty, to ask questions and
to argue his case, both with his comforters and with God. He
will not come to the situation described at the end of the book
unless he does; but the movement of deprivation, argument
and then, finally, movement onto a different plane is really
what the book is about. It gives a pattern within which life
can be found. It shows how pain must be allowed and even
owned before it is put aside and laid to rest. It cannot be
resisted or explained away. It is within this pattern of
behaviour in the face of pain that we become aware of God
and of his mercy. And it is this pattern which the book reveals
to be one of the major patterns of how human beings move
into a relationship with the mystery which is at the heart of
things.

The little Book of Jonah is a very similar case in point. In
fact in the early days of the Church it was highly valued as
the book which spoke of the resurrection. It was seen by the
first Christians as a symbolic book, one which contained,
hidden within it, the pattern of the death and rising again of
Jesus, which is after all the ultimate pattern or symbol for all
of the universe. This is how things are. In the book Jonah is
asked to go to Ninevah, a non-Jewish city, and preach to it.
His refusal leads to flight and then to tragedy. He is swallowed
up by a great fish but calls to the Lord and is vomited out
to resume his mission. The city is converted but this does not
please Jonah who still cannot understand the generosity of
God and complains that God should not be like this. But God
shades him with the leaves of a plant and asks, gently, why
this should not be. God's wish is for the whole of creation,

including the animals, to be within his peace, under the protection of his shalom. Once again the story does not, as it were, get us anywhere. It does not have a satisfactory resolution. Jonah is left sitting under his tree. But the pattern of the story is, we know, our pattern. It speaks of our call and our rejection of the call, of our death and resurrection. It also speaks of our dissatisfaction with God's disregard for the basic rules of fairness and justice as we human beings operate them. Grace is too much to cope with. So the book both mirrors and encapsulates our root experiences.

The story of Ruth exhibits the same qualities. Again it is a story which works at a number of levels. One of these levels is the one which tackles the question of how exclusive the people of God can be, for Ruth is a Moabitess. But it is also a story about us and our exclusiveness, and how that exclusiveness is overcome by love and tenderness. The setting of the story 'at the beginning of the barley harvest', with all the associations that brings of completeness and gathering in, of gleaning the fields so that nothing is forgotten, means that the story becomes a moving and luminous parable of human behaviour, and all the more compelling because it reaches down to the depths of our beings in a way which mere argumentation about who belongs and who does not could never do.

In the New Testament it is the Gospels which provide us with an archetypal pattern in the accounts they give of the life, death and rising again of Jesus of Nazareth. Obviously Christians believe that all this happened in history more or less in the way that it is told, but to believe that it happened is only to believe at one level of one's being. Christian believing is made complete when believers take this way of being, the pattern of life, death and resurrection as exhibited by Jesus, into themselves and know that they too have died and are risen with Christ. In the early church this was signified in the rite of baptism when the candidates were taken down into the water and then up and out into the church to celebrate the resurrection. They took upon themselves visibly and internally the pattern of Jesus. They not only had to believe in his life, death and resurrection but they also had to live out that pattern as believers with their lives.

Believers through the ages have testified to this and have lived through a pattern of death and resurrection in themselves. In recent times one of the most striking witnesses to this need to 'step into the pattern' of the life of Jesus is Vaclav Havel, the dissident playwright who was elected the first non-communist President of Czechoslovakia. Havel was imprisoned by the communist authorities in that country for his part in the dissident movement known as 'Charter 77'. During his imprisonment he was allowed one letter home each week. This letter was subject to very close censorship rules such as no quotation marks, no underlining, no corrections, no foreign expressions and so on. The letters were also very restricted in their content. They were limited to 'family matters' and no jokes were allowed. Partly as a consequence of these restrictions Havel's letters to his wife became a series of reflections on his life and the nature of his existence. They became a moving and profound expression of one man's encounter with the inner truth of his life. In them he speaks of the absolute importance of faith. Faith, he says,

> . . . does not draw its energy from some particular reality or assumption, on whose existence it is utterly dependent and with whose loss it would collapse like a pricked balloon. It is not a state of enchantment . . . but rather an intrinsic 'state of the spirit', a profound 'existential dimension', an inner direction . . . which . . . raises your entire existence onto a kind of higher level of Being.[4]

In one of the last letters Havel speaks of how man's very identity, his human nature, requires him to live looking towards an absolute horizon. Living in this way, says Havel, enables us to love others. Then, in the very last letter in the collection, he relates this way of living to the patterns in the Scriptures and to the pattern of life exhibited by Christ. Here he states clearly the intrinsic importance for the religious life of the Christian patterns or archetypes, and says that if we

[4]Vaclav Havel, *Letters to Olga* (Faber 1988), p. 151.

live by them then we will come to live in wholeness and freedom. He says,

> I think that religious archetypes accurately mirror the dimensions of this ambiguous essence of humanity – from the idea of paradise, that 'recollection' of a lost participation in the integrity of Being, the idea of a fall into the world as an act of 'separation' (is not the apple of knowledge in fact the 'knowledge of the self' that separates us?), the idea of the last judgement as our confrontation with the absolute horizon of our relating, right down to the idea of salvation . . .

He continues,

> Yes, man is in fact nailed down – like Christ on the cross – to a grid of paradoxes: stretched between the horizontal of the world and the vertical of Being . . . And like Christ, he is in fact victorious, but by virtue of his defeats . . . and through death – his last and greatest defeat – he finally triumphs over his fragmentation . . .[5]

This is the most remarkable testimony from one who was originally a secular playwright but who, through his reflections on the meaning of his existence in the most deprived of situations, came to a living faith in the saving patterns of Christ's life and death.

Everyday Christians, however, may find all this a little farfetched. We may struggle with all this and may find it difficult to accept that such patterns or 'archetypes' do exist deep within us. But I have come to believe that one of the major problems of being part of the twentieth century is the very fact that each one of us thinks that they are so totally unique that we are actually quite unlike each other, each one walled up, as it were, and so separate from his or her neighbour that we each have a totally unique history and a totally unique psyche. We do not believe that there are any common patterns. Everything is random. If this is one of the results of the age of reason then it is no more than a recipe for despair.

[5]Ibid., p. 375.

It ought really to be a matter of great relief for us, a real
mercy in fact, to realise that there *are* common patterns and
common values. These common and hidden inner unities do
not mean that we are all the same. Rather they show that
the way in which we may come to wholeness and to God
involves the same patterns and the practice of the same virtues. Deep within our innerness there lie ways of becoming
which all may discover and through which all may be made
whole and we may, thank God, go there together. These
patterns or myths are hidden by the business of life and are
revealed to us if we allow that business to drop away. If we
allow ourselves to follow the patterns which are then revealed
we shall be believers. The patterns which we must follow are
found within the pages of the Scriptures. What we find there
are ways of being which, when we make them our own, will
work their own magic upon us. But we have to make them
our own, or, rather, allow them to make us their own. We
have to allow them to draw us into their life.

It is perhaps for this very reason that the Ignatian way of
prayer has become so important for so many people in recent
years. The Ignatian Exercises are really a system of imaginative contemplations of Scripture passages. We are asked by St
Ignatius to take a passage of Scripture and to sit with it in
stillness and to enter into it in our imagination. We have to
imagine that we are there, to feel the dust on the road, to
hear the quarrelling of the disciples, to see Christ with our
inner eye and to allow what he says to speak to us as if we
were the one to whom it was being said. The Scripture is
thus not past but present and Christ is not a past hero but a
living Saviour. Fr Gerard Hughes has popularised this
method of praying in his book, *God of Surprises*. There he
describes the method, saying,

> Choose a passage of Scripture, read it over several times,
> focus your attention on any phrase which appeals to you,
> let this phrase hover over whatever comes to your mind
> and then speak to God as simply and as honestly as you
> can, knowing that he loves the chaos that is in you and

that his Spirit working in you can do infinitely more than you can think or imagine.[6]

It becomes clear from what Gerard Hughes and other teachers of the Ignatian method say about this particular way that they find it enables the truth about our relationship to Christ to become clear to us. If we follow through an imaginative contemplation on one of the Gospel stories and find that our reaction to Christ's words or Christ's presence is of a particular kind then we shall be able, if we are open enough, to see how we are before him. We shall know the truth of our relationship to him and be able to move on from there. In other words it is a very revealing method, one in which the word of God becomes clear to us. This is what Gerard Hughes means by 'the God of Surprises'. God is the One who speaks his word, but we cannot easily hear it. Contemplative imagination of the Scriptures and reflection on that contemplation with a spiritual guide is one of the ways in which that 'hidden word' can become clear to us. Although first put into a systematic form by Ignatius Loyola it was in existence in the Church from the beginning. It is also a method which Jung himself used to help his own patients to become more aware of their inner lives. Fr Hughes says,

> The word of God in Scripture is a special sacrament of his presence, just as real, although different in form, as his presence in the Eucharist. The words of Scripture, if we read them with faith, act like a light falling on the darkness of our inner selves so that we can find and recognise that God – Father of Abraham, Isaac and Jacob, and Father of Our Lord Jesus Christ – is also our God. I read and ponder God's action in past ages in order to recognise that same action continuing now in me.[7]

So Jung and Ignatius come together at this point in a common witness to the hidden word of God in the Scriptures. Jung tells us that we need to be in touch with the depths of

[6]Gerard W. Hughes sj, *God of Surprises* (Darton, Longman and Todd 1985), p. 49.
[7]Ibid., p. 46.

our beings, to own the shadow and to accept and live with the archetypal patterns of life which are hidden from our eyes. Ignatius shows us – as Jung also knew – that these patterns are present in the Scriptures and gives us a method by which their presence may be revealed to us and by which we may own them and live within them to our soul's health. Both show us that we need to be open to the reality of God as an affirming and life-giving presence which is hidden from our perception by our preoccupation with materialism, by our preoccupation with achievement and success, by the demands of our ego-self and by the demands of an over-rationalised style of education. Once these things are gently removed in the silent work of prayer then the hidden and loving word will emerge to bless us.

Interlude

I want to pause a moment here. The pause is to enable us to catch our breath, to think for a moment about where we have been and to let the argument sink into our consciousness.

I suspect that what I am saying may be unfamiliar and perhaps a little strange to some Christians, but that others will find that it does not go far enough. What I am suggesting is that the best way to read the Bible is not scientifically, with notes and a commentary, nor literally, as if these very words were the divinely inspired word of God. These choices are, should you be tempted to make them, both secondary. As a primary means of reading I am suggesting a third way in which the Bible is understood as carrying the hidden word of God. The Bible carries the word and carries us to the word. It contains the word within its pages and is a catalyst for our awareness of the word within ourselves and within the world all around us.

I should, perhaps, explain what I mean by 'the word of God'. God's word is permanently spoken. God utters his word and brings all things to life. But this word is hidden from us because of our preoccupations, because we answer to the demands of this world and our egos. These do not allow us to be quiet, to await and to ask God to speak his word in us. But once we do set out on this way and step into God then we will hear his word and we will know that it is uttered in us. The word will be present in us and to us as we step into the story of the people of which we are a part. It will be uttered in us also as we step into the patterns of awareness which the pages of the Bible reveal and make them our own – patterns such as the life of Moses, the exile and return to brotherhood of Joseph the dreamer, and supremely, for Christians, the life and death and rising again of Jesus of Nazareth.

This approach combines a number of traditions and insights which are often seen separately. It combines the insights of contemporary spirituality with a theology of story and the perceptions of Jung and Ignatius. It does this not to be clever or confusing, but rather because each one of these approaches has the same thing in common – a belief in the overwhelming and ever present reality of God. Each one of these approaches tries to find a way of bringing us closer to that ever present God and to the word which God utters from the foundations of the world but which is hidden from our eyes.

What we are looking for when we read the Bible is a word of salvation, a blessing as well as a truth. When we read the Bible we are looking for God and so we must step into the text as part of our greater stepping into the reality of God. This requires a certain minimum degree of trust that the text as it stands can deliver that reality to us, but at the same time a great awareness that the word of God is hidden behind or within the text and is not the text itself. This is why it is an approach which some will find difficult because it is an approach which requires a spirituality. Others will say it is not good enough because it is based on a belief that God's word is greater than these words before us. In other words this approach to reading the Bible is based upon a very 'high' doctrine of the word of God, so high that it believes that this word transcends or precedes the view that the Bible in itself is the word of God. The word of God is constantly spoken by him from all eternity and so is a living word, not a static delivered reality. In each generation it comes afresh as we find new truths and new, undiscovered directions within it.

For what has happened is that we have tamed the word of God into an easily assimilable set of truths which we can talk about in one way or another. In the Gospel stories of Jesus in the wilderness he too is beset by this temptation and answers it by saying that man shall not live by bread alone but by every word that proceeds from the mouth of God. The word is not something to talk about, a truth which we can discuss, but a reality by which we live, a force which will keep us alive, the force which does keep us alive if only we would search and allow it to live within us and then own that life.

The next section of the book is a series of studies of passages or sections of the Bible which illustrate and embody the way of seeing the Bible which the first half of the book has outlined. There are five of them, two from the Hebrew Scriptures and three from the New Testament. They are not exhaustive but simply set down out of my own reading and experiences and enthusiasms in order to encourage the reader on his or her own journey of rediscovering the hidden word. What happens when we find or are found by that word we shall consider at the end of the book.

5

'Who Told You That You Were Naked?'

(Genesis 1–3)

Let us begin with an experiment. Use your imagination for a moment to step into the Garden of Eden. In your mind's eye place yourself there. Allow yourself a little guided meditation on what it is like to be either Adam or Eve. Read through the first three chapters of Genesis and open your heart as well as your mind to the text and slowly pray through the words and the actions. Gently give yourself to your inner eye. Be in Eden.

First of all sense its beauty and its completeness.

Let your eyes wander over the colours.

Appreciate all the plants and animals, all the birds and insects.

Take delight in what you see and hear.

Rejoice in some of the complexities that make up the ways things relate to and depend upon other things in the garden.

Think how you are part of that set of relationships and how good it feels to be part of it all.

Enjoy being there.

Be aware of your own satisfaction.

Then make yourself aware of the presence of your co-inhabitant, the man or woman who is your partner in this place.

Look at them, see how beautiful they are, how finely made they are and how they are full of vigour and life.

Savour what the other person means to you, how you

feel more yourself with that person, how each of you has 'come alive' with the presence of the other.

Spend a few moments enjoying that and being thankful for it.

Then allow your consciousness to remember the part you have played in establishing the garden.

If you are the man then you can feel some satisfaction at having given identity, 'names', to all of the things in the garden.

If you are the woman then you can spend some time being glad that you personally have spoken with the other inhabitants, got to know them, established relationships with them perhaps in a different way than that open to your man-partner, and can interpret them to him.

Whether you are male or female spend a few moments remembering how you relate to the things in the garden and being glad about it.

Offer that in thanksgiving to God.

Then gently change your focus.

Turn from being aware of the garden itself to being aware of the owner.

Be aware of the one who is.

Direct your attention to the one who brought such order and beauty out of chaos.

Be aware of the one whose inspiration keeps it from falling back into chaos, who keeps it in being and who has given you your place and your life here, the one who has, as it were, let it over to you.

Think about this sustainer/owner, this creator, known as God, for a moment.

Reflect on how this sustainer/owner behaves towards you and the things in the garden.

Remember that this sustainer/owner lets you get on with things and only drops in at the end of the day to talk things over with you.

Ask yourself why God behaves like this.

Think about how friendly those conversations are and

how they seem to leave you with a greater impetus to carry on the work you are doing.

When you think about God spend a little time reflecting on some of the things that were said in the conversations – how you were given a great deal of freedom, how you could name things, talk to things and eat more or less what you wanted without restraint.

Recall how God, the sustainer/owner, said you could eat of all the fruit in the garden except one.

Spend the next few minutes being glad about God, the sustainer/owner, and the freedom God has given to you and everything else.

Offer it all to God in thanksgiving.

We could go on. But so far, so good. Let's stop for a moment and see where we have come and what we have found. Let's do a little post-meditative recollection. If this guided meditation (a technique which is increasingly used in the teaching of R.E. in schools – where it is sometimes called 'guided fantasy') has been successful, it should have demonstrated that we find a profound resonance between our lives and life in the first garden. Nothing in the meditation was in any way alien to the scriptural account and yet all of it was also to do with us today. The themes of the meditation – partnership and friendship – are contemporary themes, but partnership and friendship are also the keynotes of Eden – both between God and the creation itself but also between the two humans. What went on there and what goes on with us are intimately related. Partnership and friendship are qualities we pursue and recognise, when they occur, as having an authenticity and givenness of their own. So it is not too difficult to imagine ourselves there as one or other member of the primaeval couple, living in a place where balance and harmony, partnership and trust are the natural basis for the way things are. Moreover such a meditation is deeply refreshing. It seems to renew the well-springs of our life. When we do it we find that all of the disorganised relationships which we live with in daily life are restructured and the broken pattern of our lives is, as it were, reset.

When we use our inner eye to enter the garden we rediscover a complete symbolic relationship between male and female, between human beings and the created order and between human beings and God. That resonates with us at the most profound level. When we enter this text using our imagination and our intelligence we can find again a way of relating with God where the relationship does not depend upon dominance but on friendship. Here we can find afresh a model for the relationship between the sexes where male and female have parity and complementarity, for a number of contemporary commentaries point out the relationship between the couple is one of balance. When some English translations speak of a 'helpmate' the Hebrew means 'equal to him' or 'alongside him' which is much better translated (as in NEB) as 'partner'. Indeed the same words are used later to speak of God's relationship to human beings.

Here too we can refind a relationship between human beings and the created order where naming and stewardship replace dominance and exploitation. Indeed, some interpretations of the creation narratives go on to find in the text a prohibition on meat eating and so see the original condition of humanity to be vegetarian. Even if this is not, in the end, justifiable, there is enough to demonstrate that contemporary ways of relating to the creation which see it simply as being there for man's (and here the male pronoun is apposite) consumption are not reflected back to us in what we read.

All of this – partnership between the sexes, friendship between God and humanity, balance between human beings and the rest of the created order – all of this *can be found at some point in the text*. All of this we, today, long for. But all of this, modern life, civilisation and sometimes the church, contradict. We resonate with this text and need to return to it regularly because in a certain way our modern lifestyle has deprived us of it. When we allow ourselves to reflect prayerfully and slowly on the text we know that the first three chapters of Genesis *are about us*.

Obviously this awareness that the text is really about us is heightened for us by contemporary concerns about the creation and the increasing pressure from the scientific world

for human beings to live with rather than over against the
creation. We know we need to live with the creation as Adam
and Eve are seen to live with it. We know too that we need
to live with each other, male and female, as Adam and Eve
are seen to live with each other, and if we are believers we
know that we need to live with God in the same way that
Adam and Eve are seen to live with God, that is in interdepen-
dence and friendship. We know we need to live like this if
the created order, ourselves included, is to survive. But the
point is that even without the pressure of recent scientific
evidence of ecological damage to the created order, pressure
which has driven people back to look at the creation stories
in a new way, it would still be clear that the creation narratives are not just texts about what happened in the past but
also texts which speak to us as human beings because they
appeal to our need and longing for primal innocence. The
threat of ecological disaster throws us back to these texts
which come to us from our very beginnings and precipitates
our unspoken awareness that they are about ourselves as we
need to be. A contemporary scholar says,

> Genesis 2–3 is on one level about an individual man and
> woman. On another it is, as we have said already, about
> Man and Woman. It is about the human condition, not as
> it once was, but as it is, and as we long for it to be. It is
> written as if it was about the remote past, but it is more
> about the present and the future.[1]

But there is more to say about the results of this little
guided meditation. When we look at the text in this way we
will come to realise that many of the ways in which we have
been accustomed to read the text are false or at least seriously
misleading. They do not allow us to receive all that the text
has to give us because in a subtle and largely unseen way
they discount the links that exist between us and what is
written. They do this either by treating the text as something
to be accepted without question or viewing it as something

---

[1]Trevor Dennis, *Lo and Behold – The power of Old Testament storytelling* (SPCK
1991), p. 22.

to be studied with the disengaged mind. In this way they deprive the text of its life.

For example, if we have been taught that the text literally describes the way the universe began, then not only does that ignore what the text itself contains (i.e. two different and contradictory accounts of the sequence of events at the creation), but it also ignores the qualities of this magnificently resonant text with its refrains and repeated phrases. A reading of the text which concludes that this is how all things began is to read not just with our eyes and ears closed to the power and depth of the narrative – for this is clearly far more than mere description – but also with our eyes and ears attuned only to our own assumed needs. Indeed it is because we are listening to our own felt needs that we are insensitive to the depth and power of the narrative. If instead we engage in a slow, thoughtful, prayerful savouring of the text this will release in us the realisation that to treat it simply as a description of what happened at the beginning of things is to deny it its full worth. Moreover, not to give the text its full worth is to adopt what is known as a 'reductionist' reading of the text, that is a reading which 'reduces' its value, and ironically this is a charge which normally is laid at the door of liberal rather than fundamentalist scholars!

In a similar way a thoughtful, meditative reading of the text will also show us that these three chapters cannot be understood merely as a Hebrew version of the Babylonian creation myths, although that is also what they are. Knowing that these myths lie somewhere behind the text is interesting and helpful, especially when we see the changes which the Hebrew writers made to the older myths which reveal their different understanding of the way God works, but such knowledge in itself is not enough. More important is the fact that the narrative *engages* the hearer. It calls to us at a deeper level than that of knowledge. Its very form and strength grips us in a visceral manner and relates to who we are at depth. It is manifestly not just trying to tell us something.

Nor, least of all, can the text be understood as a primitive way of talking about the creation of the world which we, more scientifically educated people, can loftily look down on as an example of how the creation used to be explained. That would be the worst kind of interpretation, assuming that the Hebrew writers were really scientists but just did not have sufficient scientific knowledge to hand to get it right!

If we will allow ourselves to read the text slowly and thoughtfully, treating it more as if it were a piece of poetry or literature than as a piece of scientific or historical writing, then all of these false readings will dismiss themselves. They will be ruled out as evidently false and the relationship of the text to ourselves and who we are will become more apparent. In many ways it is almost because we treat the text as 'holy' or 'sacred' that we miss its true meaning for ourselves. Our respect for the text is so great that we tend to turn it into an objective 'thing' which stands over against us and which we have to understand or obey or be subject to. Instead we need to see the text in a much more personal way, as something of which we are a part, or which is part of us. We need to see it as something like a layer in our psychic consciousness, a story which, when read, delivers us into the hand of God. When we read the first three chapters of Genesis in this way, then we will know that it is a text about us as human beings and about our deep-seated awareness of, as well as our need to be restored to, our original condition.

Let us go back to the text and see how this works in practice. Read through the first chapter of Genesis again and go on until chapter 2 verse 4. Stop at that point for the time being. We will deal with chapters 2 and 3 in a moment. This time, as you read, instead of allowing yourself to be drawn into Eden itself, as if this were a guided meditation, let yourself be led by the sense of the text. As you read ask yourself the question *Where is the text taking me?* If we do this and allow the text to accomplish its own work then I believe that we shall see more than we have hitherto allowed ourselves to see.

In chapter 1 the text develops a rhythm as the days of the week succeed each other and the refrain comes, 'And there was evening and there was morning, the fourth . . . fifth . . . sixth day.' This is then immediately followed by the sequence, 'And God said, "Let there be . . ." ' Most of us have heard these words often enough in church but they never seem to lose their resonance. The sequences roll on through the different parts of the creation – water, land, heavens, sun, moon, fish, birds, cattle and creeping things – until we reach the creation of man. Many Christian commentators assume that the climax of these sequences comes at the end of the chapter when we read (v. 26). 'Then God said, "Let us make humankind in our image . . ."'. The impression that this is the climax is heightened by the artificial chapter divisions in the Christian Bible which mean a new chapter – unwarranted by the Hebrew text – begins at the end of the sixth day and the creation of humankind. But the true climax to the narrative is found in the first three verses of chapter 2,

> Thus the heavens and the earth were finished, and all their multitude. And on the seventh day God finished the work that he had done, and he rested on the seventh day from all the work that he had done. So God blessed the seventh day and hallowed it, because on it God rested from all the work that he had done in creation.

At this point the narrative breaks and begins the cycle all over again, this time in an entirely different style.

So the climax of the first creation narrative is not the creation of man but the creation of the sabbath and the institution of 'rest' as a sign of the sabbath. This becomes clear when the text is read slowly and the rhythms and sequences of phrase allowed to exercise their full force upon the reader. Judaism, of course, has preserved this insight, but the traditional Christian view, at least in the Western Church, has been that the climax of the account is the creation of humankind. This way of seeing things is extremely hard to eradicate. Contemporary Christian commentators unwittingly keep this traditional, but highly anthropocentric view alive when they make much of how the first creation narrative ends with the creation of the human species, male and female together, and the commandment to stewardship. This is seen, rightly, as a parable of partnership between the sexes, and between humanity and the created order, but it is then contrasted very unfavourably with the second account of the creation (2:4b–24) where man is created first and given the care of the garden and woman is created last out of the man's rib. However attractive this is as a non-sexist interpretation it is another misunderstanding.

The first account does not end with the creation of man and woman but with the creation of the sabbath. Nor is the second account as chauvinist as is often implied because it is here that woman is described as a 'partner' and the mutuality of the relationship between the man and the woman, who shall 'become one flesh', is very clear. The second account is perhaps better seen as a further deepening, this time in terms of a personal drama, of what the first account expresses in poetic and elegaic terms. But the point for the moment is that the climax of the first section is the creation of the sabbath.

The Jewish community keeps this alive within itself. There the sabbath is understood as the renewal of creation and its observance provides the opportunity to be reminded of the original blessing conferred by God upon all things. The blessing is celebrated and the community reminded of the original purpose of all things. On the sabbath humanity is recalled to its proper place and reminded of how it has to care for things and to steward what it has been given. All this Judaism preserves. You can see this in the different ways in which the two communities reflect upon these texts publicly. If we were to listen to a sermon on Genesis 1 in a synagogue there is no doubt that the sabbath would figure in it prominently. A sermon on the same text in a Christian church would more likely be an attempt to show how creation can be compatible with evolution! The place and importance of the sabbath as a sign of restoration, rest and blessing is markedly absent, particularly in the more Protestant churches where work and duty are emphasised. In other words the Christian tradition is still in thrall to the effects of the Reformation and the Enlightenment, grappling with an overburdened conscience and the effects of rationalism.

Some contemporary Christian scholars have begun, however, to see that they need to return to the older tradition at this point. In particular Jurgen Moltmann is very clear about the centrality of the sabbath in the creation narratives. He says,

The goal and completion of every Jewish and every Christian doctrine of creation must be the doctrine of the sabbath; for on the sabbath and through the sabbath God 'completed' his creation, and on the sabbath and through it, men and women perceive as God's creation the reality in which they live and which they themselves are. The sabbath opens creation for its true future. On the sabbath the redemption of the world is celebrated in anticipation. The sabbath is itself the presence of eternity in time, and a foretaste of the world to come.[2]

He goes on,

It is the sabbath which manifests the world's identity as creation, sanctifies and blesses it.[3]

Moltmann also criticises the neglect of this understanding in the western Church where the impression is given that when Jesus healed the sick on the sabbath he repealed the sabbath commandment altogether. God's essence is then seen in terms of his 'creativity' and men and women, who are made in God's image and likeness, thereby discover their essence when they are active and 'creative'. We have only to recall the number of groups – especially church groups – which are in existence urging us all to be 'creative', to know the truth of this remark. Moltmann urges us all to recover the importance of rest and delight rather than frenetic 'creativity' as central concepts for understanding God and humankind. He says, 'In the sabbath stillness men and women no longer intervene in the environment through their labour. They let it be entirely God's creation. They recognise that as God's property creation is inviolable . . .'[4] The important contribution Moltmann makes is to force us to move away from seeing humanity, especially the male gender, as the climax of God's creative activity. Creation is made for the sabbath. Equally important is Moltmann's emphasis on the

[2]Jurgen Moltmann *God in Creation – An ecological doctrine of creation* (SCM 1985), p. 276.
[3]Ibid., p. 276.
[4]Ibid., p. 277.

centrality of 'rest' and 'delight' rather than constant activity as central to the nature of God and hence to the humanity which is made in God's likeness. This is all a welcome shift. The shift is continued by another, more recent Christian scholar, who says,

> Thus each sabbath, each seventh day, is declared blessed time . . . To step inside its boundaries is to find oneself in God's time, enjoying God's rest . . . To observe it is to keep the rhythms of creation. It is as natural as can be, and far away from the pinched, burdensome thing that Christians have sometimes made of it. In my experience Jews understand it better and find it easier to observe in the proper spirit.[5]

However that may be – and it is certainly less true now than it was that Christians regard the sabbath as pinched and burdensome – it should be clear that the creation narrative is still about us at this point. It is about us and our activity, about us as belonging ultimately to a sabbath existence rather than a work existence; it is about our daily attitudes to ourselves and what we have. The text is not history. And this continues to be the case as the narrative moves into Genesis 2 and 3.

Genesis 2 sets the scene for the crisis which unravels itself in chapter 3. In chapter 2 the garden is laid out and the man is placed in it. The tree of life is introduced as are the beasts and the birds of the air. Then woman appears. All that has been said so far is description. Now the stage is set. At this point the psychological depths begin to appear. We are suddenly plunged into a different order of things, just like a change of key in Mozart. For the writer says, 'And the man and his wife were both naked, and were not ashamed.' The words '. . . and were not ashamed' ring a warning after the long process of stage setting. The words '. . . and were not ashamed' are deliberately placed at this crucial point in order to prepare us for what is to come. The man and the woman are portrayed as open, totally without defence, unequipped,

---

[5]Dennis, op. cit., p. 12.

not just in terms of clothes but also in terms of psychological property. They are unashamed of what they are, they are 'naked' in the psychological sense of the word. Naked at this point does not mean 'nude'. Nude is an entirely modern word. 'Naked' means that they were without self-knowledge. The text says that they were naked but not ashamed, meaning that their lack of shame was quite 'unknowing'. It is not that they knew that they were naked but did not care, or did not feel ashamed of it. They simply did not know they were naked. Their nakedness is simply what was the case for them. They did not know that they were naked and so could not be ashamed or, in a different sense, unashamed. They had not begun to make any sort of interior or personal judgement about their state at all. It was simply how they were.

But that very statement in the text, with all of its implications, immediately announces to the reader that something is going to happen which involves their nakedness and their lack of shame. The man and the woman are about to be exposed to a situation in which their nakedness will be the central factor in some sort of crisis. What this crisis is begins to be apparent during a conversation between the woman and the serpent about the trees in the garden. This is really a conversation about knowledge and lack of knowledge. By encouraging the woman to eat of the fruit of the tree the serpent introduces the woman to the question of whether she wants to have knowledge or not. The woman is 'naked', psychologically untainted, fresh and unaware of any difficulty even if she does eat the fruit; fresh and unaware of any trap set for her by the serpent. In her nakedness she does not see any harm in having the knowledge which eating the apple will give her and so she disobeys and eats. The woman thinks that the knowledge of wisdom is just the same sort of thing as food. The fruit of the tree was good to eat, good to look at and would, moreover, give you knowledge. What was the harm in that? And in one sense she was right, there was no harm. Nothing physically disastrous would happen to her at all. The serpent was right, she would not die. What happened was that she was given knowledge. And this is part of the wonder and depth of the story, for there is a profound sense

in which it is not simply the act of choosing to eat the fruit
of the tree which, whatever Christian tradition may have
made of it since, is the key issue. As we shall see it is not
disobedience in itself which leads to loss of blessedness. The
question is more complex than that.

What happens after the woman and then the man eat of
the fruit of the tree is that they come to know that they are
naked. They are given knowledge. Whereas before they did
not 'know' that they were naked, now they do. The crucial
question then becomes what they should do with that knowledge when they acquire it, for it was told them that when
they had knowledge they would be like God. So the crucial
question is not whether they did or did not eat the apple, but
what they are to do with the knowledge that eating the apple
gives them. The question is whether the man and the woman
can *own* what has happened and accept it. It is their refusal
or lack of ability to accept what they have been given rather
than their disobedience which leads to their banishment. The
real question they have been posed is, 'Can they bear the gift
of being like God and the risk it contains or will they flinch
and hide from that risk and the One who is its source?'

The answer becomes clear in one of the most moving and
crucial passages in the whole of Scripture. The man and the
woman, having been given knowledge of their nakedness,
cannot accept it. They make aprons and cover themselves.
In the cool of the day God walks in the garden and calls to
them, but they not only hide their nakedness, they also hide
themselves. God calls, 'Where are you?' And when we hear
this call we know that it is not simply a call to Adam but
also a call to all of us at all points in time. It is not simply a
call to say where we are physically, it is a call which reaches
down into the very depths of our being, down into the very
bowels of our hidden self. It cuts across all of our disguises,
reaches through all of our protestations and asks, gently but
firmly, where we really are. It is the word of God calling us
out, asking us whether we can bear to turn and face the one
who loves us. Eventually Adam answers and comes out to
face God, speak the truth and confess his fear. And the question comes, 'Who told you that you were naked?' Once again

this is an existential question which resonates within us. It is ultimately a question about being, about exposure before the divine, about our vulnerability, about choices and the anguish in them. In one sense nobody has told Adam that he is naked. He discovered for himself that his nakedness was more than nudity when he ate the fruit. He knew about his total nakedness when he gained his knowledge. For behind the question lie further questions about the difference between life and death, being and non-being.

First of all the question 'Who told you that you were naked?' is a question about contentment. What is being asked is why Adam was not content with his original state, his primal innocence, his original blessing, his 'nakedness' given to him at the beginning of things. The first thing that God was asking is why it was that the man and the woman were not content with their created state so that they had to disobey and eat the fruit. And the answer to that question is, strangely enough, one which only God himself can provide. The question must be turned around and God must be asked why the tree of the knowledge of good and evil is there at all. If we are supposed to be content with our original condition then why does God provide the occasion for discontent by planting the tree and forbidding the eating of its fruit? If we are to be rebuked for discontent then why was temptation so clearly placed in our way? Could it be that God wanted Adam and Eve to eat and discover their nakedness and come to be like God, with the possession of knowledge? Many have asked this question and concluded that the expulsion from the garden is not accidental, due to our own mismanagement and stupidity, but provided for, expected, willed almost, by God himself. As one contemporary rabbi has concluded – we did not fall, we were pushed.

But also in this question, 'Who told you that you were naked?' another question is hidden. And this is the question of confidence. Both our contentment and our confidence are being tested. But the confidence which is being tested is the confidence we have once our nakedness has been discovered. In this sense the question becomes 'Who told you that nakedness, once you knew you had it, was something to be ashamed of?' Here, then, is God's call to individuation. In this sense knowledge of our nakedness represents maturity. Maturity, what Jung calls individuation, means accepting our knowledge of nakedness, owning it and recognising that it is a blessing – because it will involve us in responsible choices – rather than something to be ashamed of. This, rather than the unashamed, womb-like innocence of Eden, is the true condition of humanity. Looked at in this way the tree once again becomes God's gift and the drama in the garden is the drama of whether, once the man and the woman know that they are naked, they can accept, and own and bear the gift. Not surprisingly they find the knowledge they have been given too much for them and they hide, both from the knowledge itself and from the one who gives it. As the psalmist says, 'Such knowledge is too high for me and I cannot attain unto it'.

So God's question to Adam 'Who told you that you were naked?' is *the* existential question. It is asked of every human being and has to be answered if that human being is to come to maturity and individuation. Asking about nakedness is the way divinity has of talking about the need for us to own who we are and to accept that the way to our maturity lies through mature acceptance of the knowledge of good and evil and the inescapable necessity of making choices about good and evil. This is why, in the end, Adam and Eve have to leave the garden and make their way in the world, the place of choice and redemption. For the Garden of Eden is paradise, it is not this world. It is the place of not-knowing, the place of innocence. It is the place where we do not know about our nakedness and where we are not ashamed. God does not want us to stay there. Indeed God cannot let us stay there without denying his own nature and without denying us the possibility of reaching a state where we have a free relationship with him, where we stand and look at him as free sons and daughters who share and claim and own the responsibility of knowledge. That is what God wants and so he removes us from the garden where we have no knowledge and no shame.

But to say this, which is both to dispense humanity from an archetypal and ineradicable guilt and to deny that God would have kept us like innocent children in our original play-pen, flies in the face of much conventional thinking. At this point Christians might listen with profit to a contemporary Jewish scholar, Jonathan Magonet, who says,

> But if it is a liberation, however bitter and painful it may be at the moment of separation, then human beings travel bearing a full responsibility for their life and their actions . . . And in terms of the biblical faith, they also have the ultimate freedom – to choose or not to choose God, and that in the end is what the adventure begun with Abraham is all about . . . Perhaps it is the fear of that freedom that has led human beings so often to impose their own chains, often religious chains, upon themselves and others, rather than face the loneliness and demands such a challenge imposes.[6]

But that is not quite the end of the matter. The man and the woman cannot stay in the garden of innocence. They have to go, and they cannot return. '. . . and at the east of the garden of Eden he placed the cherubim, and a sword flaming and turning to guard the way to the tree of life.' There is no way back into the garden except the way out. Indeed, if we did not accept this then there would be no story and, effectively, no redemption. God calls us to love him through the tragedy of life and across the sea of despair and not without it. We have actually to be redeemed. We have actually to travel all of the way. We have actually to pass through the waters of the Red Sea and allow our sins to flounder behind us as the water comes back to cover our steps. We cannot but travel through the wilderness and put our faith in the pillar of cloud by day and the pillar of fire by night. The only ways back to where we have come from are through and by means of the cross and the resurrection. This does not mean simply believing that the cross saves but accepting the reality of the cross in one's life and living the death of Christ until he come.

There is much in modern thinking which cannot accept the

[6]Jonathan Magonet, *A Rabbi's Bible* (SCM 1990), p. 115.

existence of the angel with the flaming sword and insists that the best way to God is the way back. I suspect this to be a reaction against the violence of life in today's world, a reversion to apparent simplicities in the face of so much that is insoluble. But it is remarkable that this same 'New Age' thinking which believes that if only we could see it all would be well, is also very apolitical, unable or unwilling to indulge in politics. This is again an indication of an isolationism, a lack of willingness to struggle to put things right, a hesitancy before the complexities which God has given us to struggle with, both within ourselves and within the world. In the end it is a failure of nerve, but also a failure of theology; a failure to see that the very weft and warp of life has to be made good and that we have a place and a responsibility in that process. The quest for social justice cannot be laid aside because it is a co-operation in the work of God who is continually redeeming the world. To lay this quest aside is to assume implicitly that we can turn back to the garden and the angel with the flaming sword is no longer there. But it is also to assume implicitly that we ourselves, as individuals, do not need the redeeming work of God. Indeed, it is to assume that we were removed from the garden for no good reason and should, by rights, be back there, talking with God in the cool of the evening and not crying out to him from the ovens of Auschwitz or the killing fields of Pol Pot.

A number of modern thinkers are beginning to see that Christians have really made mountains out of molehills as far as some parts of the stories in Genesis are concerned. In one sense far too much has been made of it all. This is particularly true in so far as some doctrines of original sin are concerned. In modern terms, what is described in the early pages of Genesis is humankind's refusal to be mature. We are sure that we can redeem ourselves. This is really a fall of a different kind from that envisaged by the traditional form of the doctrine of original sin. It is rather a fall into ego, a fall into the capacity to trust our separate selves and the powers of these separate selves. Ego, however, divides us from our true end, it encourages us to think of ourselves as separate; necessarily separate beings who can control and subjugate everything that is. The turning away from ego, the movement out of hiding to face the one who calls, is the beginning of wisdom.

Bede Griffiths, a Christian monk who now lives in India in an ashram devoted to unity, says,

> The human mind as we experience it thinks always in terms of duality, of subject and object, of mind and matter, of truth and error, and everything is perceived in terms of time and space . . . Yet there is always something within us which yearns for unity, which is in search of the lost Paradise . . . [7]

He goes on,

> But there is no simple way to return. An angel with a flaming sword stands in the way . . . The only way forward lies through suffering and death . . . It is through suffering and death that confidence in this world and in the triumphs of the rational mind is broken and humanity learns to surrender to God . . .[8]

[7]Bede Griffiths, *A New Vision of Reality* (Collins 1989), p. 100.
[8]Ibid., p. 101.

6

The Uses of Adversity
(Genesis 37–50)

The story of Joseph begins before Joseph was born. It begins with Jacob and Rachel, or even before that. It begins with Jacob and Rachel because Jacob loved Rachel more than he loved Leah, and Joseph was Rachel's child, not Leah's. That is the beginning of it. The consequence was that Jacob loved Joseph more than any other of his children. The stated cause for this was that Joseph was the child of his old age, but it was also, although the Bible does not say it in so many words, because he was Rachel's child. Jacob had loved Rachel and after her death he seems to have transferred to Joseph, and perhaps also to Benjamin her second and last child, the love which he had for her. Favouritism of one child over another runs through these chapters like a golden thread. Joseph, then, was a spoilt child, given a coat of many colours (or 'a long-sleeved coat') by his father. He lorded it over his brothers who were born of mothers whom his father had not loved. Because of his insufferable and unrestrained egotism his brothers remove him from the family by deceit and so set in motion a drama of redemption.

The story as we have it in the Bible has an inner and an outer drama. The outer drama is the wondrous, magical tale of how Joseph is sold into slavery but always turns tragedy into success until at the last he surfaces from prison to become second only to Pharaoh, as a man of immense power who is then able to deliver his brothers and his father from famine. The inner drama is found in the story of how Joseph himself comes to accept both the blessing and the curse which Jacob's favouritism had contained but to redeem the curse and use the blessing. It is the drama of how Joseph moved through the intense darkness, guilt and suffering engendered when families destroy themselves because of power, jealousy and violence, out into the great unbreakable strength and grace which only come when that power and jealousy are owned and redeemed and brought to good use as the very means of reconciliation. It is a story of how, through the hand of God (although God is never a visible protagonist in the drama), nothing is ever wasted. At the end Joseph is able to say to his brothers, 'Do not be afraid! Am I in the place of God? Even though you intended to do harm to me, God intended it for good, in order to preserve a numerous people, as he is doing today.'[1] Julian of Norwich, in her meditations on the nature of pain so many hundreds of years later, says the same thing when she writes, '. . . when we come up and receive that sweet reward which grace has made for us, there we shall thank and bless our Lord, endlessly rejoicing that we ever suffered woe',[2] and Meister Eckhardt, writing not long before, says that suffering is the swiftest steed to bring us to perfection. That is what the Joseph story is all about. Let us now see how it all unfolds.

The best way to do this is to read the text in a different way. Rather than reading the text as we would usually do, caught up in the pace and intensity of the narrative, we should try to read it differently, this time with an awareness of the different themes or images which recur throughout that narrative. Literary scholars call these *leitmotiven* or 'leading themes'. The Bible is particularly rich in these themes and they recur almost wherever you allow the page to fall open. The same ones can be found in books from vastly different periods and vastly different origins. Unfortunately they have to a large extent been ignored by biblical scholars who have concentrated on other questions, such as the historical credibility of the narrative or the need to distinguish between the different authors of a single piece of narrative. But as we found when reading the creation stories in the Book of Genesis, a

---

[1] Genesis 50:19–20.
[2] Julian of Norwich, *Showings*, The Long Text, ch. 48.

slower and more meditative way of reading the text puts us into touch with different, deeper layers of meaning than those uncovered by the 'excavation' techniques of modern scholarship. This also brings the text alive once again for the modern consciousness. Reading the text differently reveals hidden secrets. When a slower and more meditative approach is adopted then, among other things, we become aware of the deeper, inner themes which the text carries. If we do this, letting the phrases go slowly through our minds, allowing the different word clusters and images to resonate within us, then a number of the *leitmotiven* which are hidden below the surface will become apparent.

One of the themes easiest to spot is favouritism. We have already seen how favouritism, especially the favouritism of a child by one or other of the parents, has been a predominant motif in the story so far. Rebekah loved Jacob more than she loved Esau and so engineered the deception of Isaac in favour of the younger son. Favouritism continues to colour the Joseph story right to the end. Favouritism is the blessing and the curse which afflicts Joseph. But the story is not just about the favouritism shown to Joseph by Jacob. At a deeper level it is also about the favouritism of God and how that undermines and subverts human systems with both its arbitrariness but also its grace. This becomes clearer at the very end of the story. By then one might have expected the initial favouritism to be resolved by the reconciliation which is effected between Joseph and his brothers and the arrival of the aged Jacob in Egypt. This would have fulfilled our natural desire to see the evil effects of favouritism corrected and proper justice done. But just as it is coming to an end the story surprises us yet again by revealing that this issue is by no means closed. Even at the death of Jacob, when Joseph brings his children to him to bless as he is dying, Jacob blesses the younger rather than the elder with his right hand and so Ephraim is marked out for greatness over against the older son, Manasseh. At one level the story-teller is obviously enjoying a joke against his hearers who were thinking that everything was coming to a righteous conclusion. But the twist to the tale also pointedly reminds us, just as we were about to settle back and say, effectively, all's well that ends well, that the story is about God's ways rather than our own. The whole narrative, we are told in this last scene, is a drama about how the blessing of God is given by God to whom he wills and cannot be predetermined by human laws of inheritance. It is a narrative of how human beings rebel against the apparent injustice of God's blessing but how God is continually at work weaving his own patterns within the warp and weft of our lives, bringing his good out of our evil.

That is not the end of the matter. Rachel's second child, whose birth brought about her death, was Benjamin. He too was a favourite and he plays a crucial role in the drama of reconciliation between Joseph and his brothers at the end of the story. It is as if Joseph, knowing that Jacob's favouritism of him as a young man had been the cause of his exile, uses Benjamin, the remaining favourite son, to remind his brothers of what they had done. Joseph uses Benjamin to point up the reality that he, Joseph, now has the power to do to them what they had once done to him. But somehow we, the readers, know that in the end he will not do it. We are somehow aware that he has journeyed not just to Egypt but also through some terrible but transforming experience which holds him back from destruction. Something has delivered him from the need to be revenged. We know that and perhaps Joseph knows it, but of course the brothers do not. Benjamin, the remaining favourite, becomes the focus for the realisation by the brothers that the cycle of destruction which favouritism had unleashed, has, at least for the time being, been broken. The hiding of the silver cup in Benjamin's sack is a teasing reminder to the brothers that the favourite might also be the victim, and this is the trigger for the return of the brothers to Joseph and the final climax where Judah opens himself to Joseph, not knowing he was Joseph, and so brings them all back together.

The point is that favouritism remains an essential element throughout the narrative. It is not pushed away, it is not discarded as ultimately a sinful act which must, in all good stories, especially religious ones, be put right. Rather it is a source of irony in the narrative. In the end it is turned around and seen to be an instrument of redemption. The favouritism that God has exercised through Jacob towards Joseph is not overthrown but becomes a source of blessing for them all. The cycle of deceit and violence is not held at bay but acknowledged, owned and used. In doing this Joseph displays enormous self-possession, strength beyond expectations. He has not sought revenge but grasped the shadow which has haunted them all and allowed it to work for good.

Much the same could be said of another of the *leitmotiven* in the story, this time the theme of deceit. As we have already seen this theme is entwined with the theme of favouritism. It first entered into the life-blood of the family in Abraham's deception of Isaac on Mount Moriah, just as, perhaps, the recurrent favouritism began with Sarah's jealousy of Hagar and the son that Hagar bore to Abraham before Isaac. The capacity for deception remains within the characters in the story like a hidden virus. It is eventually used by Jacob to secure the birthright and is used by him and upon him – especially during his stay with Laban – throughout his life. But it is his favourite son Joseph, the victim of deception, who ultimately uses deception to redeem the family from its power. He has learned, through his descent into Egypt and his sufferings in slavery and prison, that somehow the power of deception has to be broken. The Bible only hints at Joseph's inner journey away from the apparently inevitable cycle of deception. One of these hints occurs when he is faced with the attempt of Potiphar's wife to seduce him and deceive her husband. Joseph resists this, according to the text, with quiet strength. At the end of the story he has come to the point where he is even able to use deception with great skill and control to show his family how they have been in its grip but may now be released from it. Ultimately, then, Joseph is their redeemer.

But supremely he is his own self-redeemer. We can see this when we look at another of the *leitmotiven* which are scattered through the story, this time the motif of *bowing down*. As we have already said, Joseph's troubles are rooted in the past and in his father's love for Rachel above Leah. But Joseph is not free from this past as we can see when he dreams and tells his brothers his dreams. The first is the dream about the sheaves of corn where his sheaf stood upright but his brothers' sheaves gathered around 'and bowed down to my sheaf'. The same thing happens in the second dream, where '. . . the sun, the moon and eleven stars were bowing down to me'. The brothers naturally interpret the dreams as evidence of Joseph's desire that they, who were simply the children of their father's loins and not of their father's love, should bow down to him in real life. They assume the dreams to be a form of wish-fulfillment, just as, for all we know, Joseph does at this point. But this somewhat Freudian view is not all that can be said about dreams in general or these dreams in particular. These dreams are also evidence of some deeper reality hidden away in Joseph's psyche, of which he is as yet unaware. They are evidence of something going on within him which he has not yet come to terms with. The dreams are not so much about his unfulfilled desires as about the power of his personality, which as yet he cannot either acknowledge or own because it is too threatening. All he can do at this point is to become aware, through the dreams, that some struggle is going on within him and to project that struggle, with inevitably disastrous consequences, into his own situation. One of the underlying themes of the Joseph story is the process by which he comes to know about the inner reality of these dreams, and befriends and uses their apparently destructive reality not just without harm to himself but also to the benefit of his brothers and the greater good of the whole people of Egypt.

After the initial dreams we hear nothing more of 'bowing down' until much later, at the point where Joseph has been taken out of prison by Pharaoh and made his chief minister. Pharaoh gives him unprecedented power and decks him in the finest linen and places him in his second chariot. '. . . and they cried out in front of him, "Bow the knee!" '³ And with that sudden reiteration of the word 'bow' it is as if things begin to fall into place and we can begin to see what has been happening in the inner drama of the story. Something has happened to the use of the word 'bow'. It certainly reminds

³Genesis 41:43.

us of the dreams but this time its meaning is not the same. It does not carry the negative implications it did earlier in the story. Somehow and somewhere it has been owned. And then a page or so later, when Joseph's brothers are sent by his father to Egypt to buy grain, these glimmerings come together and we suddenly understand. The text says, 'And Joseph's brothers came and bowed themselves before him with their faces to the ground.'[4] Then we know that this is all part of the way the story is working out in reverse, for it continues, 'Joseph also remembered the dreams that he had dreamed about them.'[5] But this is not the end of it. When the brothers return to Egypt a second time, this time with Benjamin, and are taken to Joseph's house to eat with him the text reads again, '. . . they . . . bowed to the ground before him.'[6] At that point Joseph must have been reminded of the past once more for he asks them about the welfare of their father. Again they bow their heads. Then again, when they are brought back to Joseph after the cup has been discovered in Benjamin's sack, 'they fell to the ground before him.'[7]

This recurrent theme with the repeated words, 'they bowed down to him', is, of course, deeply ironic. The irony is contained, first of all, in the way Joseph's dream is fulfilled, but fulfilled in a way he did not initially expect. Neither we as the readers, nor Joseph as the protagonist, can avoid being aware of this. The words themselves, 'bow down', are repeated like a refrain in a poem, and the text itself points up the irony of the strange fulfillment when it says that Joseph remembered the dreams which he had. But the irony is also contained in the fact that this time Joseph does not destroy the brothers as they had destroyed him. At the end of his journey he is able to break the power that his egotism has had over him. Originally he was unable to break this power because it was able to boost his ego. As a young man the dreams had been proof to him of his supremacy. Now he has

[4]Genesis 42:6.
[5]Genesis 42:9.
[6]Genesis 43:26.
[7]Genesis 44:14.

been purged of the evil of egotism but is still able to remain who he is, a powerful man of exceptional ability. Now that his journey has freed him from the need to boost and protect his innate power he is able to exercise compassion and openness towards those who had persecuted him. He knows that what had happened to him was of God and he says so. He is able to use the force which had once been his downfall to be the agency of redemption. The phrase 'bow down' is used throughout the narrative as a signal, a signal which triggers within the reader or hearer awareness of how egotism can be used for good but must first be transmuted into good.

For the clear pattern of Joseph's life is that he cannot be defeated by circumstances. This is the major leitmotif which colours his career. He always claims, seemingly with ease, the blessing of greatness. He is put in the pit but not allowed to die. He is sold into slavery but bought by Potiphar, the captain of the guard. He is put in prison for allegedly seducing Potiphar's wife but is able to tell the meaning of dreams and so come to the ear of Pharaoh. He becomes Pharaoh's chief minister. The leitmotif this time – clearly implied if not stated – is, 'The Lord was with Joseph and he became a successful man . . .'. But once again this 'success' which so threatens to overwhelm, and which in so many other places in the Bible does overwhelm, is used by Joseph to bring peace and plenty where there was, or could have been, disaster. In economic terms he uses it to keep so many people alive who would otherwise die of famine. He is shown not as the selfish potentate but as the wise prince, keeping wealth for the good of all, and not just those in Egypt. In personal terms he is portrayed as one who uses his success to reward those who had conspired against him. Now he is able to claim the blessing and perceive that the purpose of the blessing is that others should be blessed through him.

By the time we have read the story slowly and allowed all of its nuances and hidden linkages to work their magic on our inner being, another question, if we are thoughtful, may come into our mind. We may have begun to wonder how such a story arose. Where did it come from? How 'true' is it? What is its real origin? The commentaries will give us a

number of answers. They will tell us that there is some historical evidence for Semitic tribes being given grazing rights in
parts of Egypt at certain periods, and so there may well have
been Hebrews in the court of the Pharaohs. They will also
tell you of Egyptian legends upon which the Joseph story may
have been based. A recent, more sophisticated, but controversial suggestion about the origins of the story is found in a
Jewish commentary on Joseph where the author suggests that
the writer of the narrative sees in Joseph a prototype of
King David who was the source of blessing for Judah.[8] The
suggestion is that the writer is a woman at the court of
Solomon. She, in support of the house of David, portrays
Joseph as the one who, like David, had claimed the blessing
of God and used it to the blessing of the nation. It is certainly
true that both Joseph and David share a heightened sense of
'blessing' and both have the boldness to claim and accept the
blessing which God gives. Each of them accepts the repeated
pattern of success which comes their way and the blessing of
God which such success indicates to be present. It could well
be that the author of the textual strand in the Pentateuch
known to scholars as 'J', which includes the Joseph stories,
was, if not a woman, somebody who wished to find Davidic
prototypes in the history of the people.

But my own feeling is that however correct such analyses
prove to be, or however accurate they are in their uncovering
of the historical sources of the text in question, they miss the
real point. The real point is that the source of the Joseph
story lies within the human psyche. It arises from the depths
of the human personality and has a timeless appeal precisely
because it speaks about who we are at root. We have already
had hints of this as we have read the text and discovered its
leading themes. The story of Joseph and his brothers begins
in history but it also describes the archetypal patterns which
are present within human relationships and the processes
which human beings must undergo if they wish to come to
maturity. In other words although the story has historical
beginnings, whether or not it is historically true is of little

[8]Rosenberg and Bloom, *The Book of J* (Faber 1990).

religious significance. The story is above all *psychologically* true, and so by being psychologically true it is about all of us and how we find God as well as about Joseph and how he found God.

A modern thinker who has written a great deal about the psychological truth of the 'stories' of the Hebrew Bible is an American, John Sanford. In his book about Jacob, Joseph and Moses he puts all this very clearly when he says,

> We can be sure that questions of historicity and credibility did not trouble the ancient Hebrews who first told and listened to these tales. For them, these ancient stories became part of the fabric of their souls, affecting them at a deep level of their being; they were sacred tales to be preserved for all time. When stories do this, it is because they bear an unconscious, as well as a conscious, meaning. This happens whenever a story is archetypal, that is, when it carries within it a meaning that is typical and universal for all humanity. Mythology, fairy tales and the ancient stories from the Bible are all archetypal; they all have a power to affect us through the unconscious by stimulating and arousing in us the living imagery of the soul. These stories have power because they tell us how it always has been and always will be with human beings. That being so, they affect us, even when they are not rationally understood.[9]

That is a splendid summary of how we ought to understand and read the Bible, but it applies to the story of Joseph in particular. Joseph is an archetypal figure. The Jewish scholar who thought that the writer saw in Joseph a prototype of David was right to a certain extent. Joseph *is* a prototype, but not just of David. He is also a prototype of all those who are, in one way or another, whether with or against their will, drawn into the process of redemption through suffering. What happened to him is always happening and will continue to happen. It is a parable of how things are and of how

[9]John Sanford, *The Man Who Wrestled With God* (Paulist Press 1987), p. 5.

redemption happens. That is why so many Christians see in Joseph something of a prototype of Jesus.

Perhaps we can just remind ourselves of how all this works out. In the story, as we have already seen, Joseph goes through a process of maturation. In psychological terms he moves out of individualism into individuation. He begins as someone who is concerned with his own prowess and position but ends up as someone who is the epitome of wisdom, serving others with his power and authority, conscious of his own value and worth but unwilling and to a certain extent now unable, because of what he had been through, to abuse that power and authority. This is shown first in the little vignette of his dealings with Potiphar's wife and then in the extended account of his dealings with his brothers. In the process of redeeming himself he becomes able to redeem others. It would have been very easy for Joseph, with the egocentric personality that he had, to have become full of self-pity. He could have lamented his fate and wallowed in feelings of being sorry for himself at a number of points along his journey. But for reasons which we can only begin to guess at, he did not. He remained singularly open to the view that God was at work in all of his adventures. We are often told, during the story, that 'God was with Joseph' and usually this phrase is placed in the text at points when Joseph's fortunes are reversed and he is brought out of darkness. But read in another way the phrase is equally evidence of the fact that Joseph has remained open to God and has been patient in tribulation. He seemed to have remained convinced that God was at work in the situation even though what God was doing was not particularly visible. God was with him but could not be seen to be with him. In the end it is this constant sense of Joseph's dependence upon God at work *in the mystery of existence* that gives the story so much of its power.

The text provides very few clues as to exactly why Joseph was able to be faithful in this way. Nor should we expect it to do so. The Hebrew writers were not psychologists in the same manner as us moderns. The story actually fares better for not having passages where Joseph's inner development is minuted in detail. Like so much in the Hebrew Bible it is a text of great subtlety and strength not because it is unaware of the interiority of the protagonists – it manifestly is – but because it hints at that interiority. It comes at these questions slant, leaving the reader aware of the complexities and depths but also aware that these complexities cannot be codified or brought too near the light without destroying them completely.

Although Joseph must have been haunted by ambiguities and lack of perspective from the very beginning, he nonetheless comes through into a natural and strong faithfulness which enables him to reach through to those who had wronged him so dreadfully. John Sanford relates this capacity to be faithful within great difficulty to Joseph's discovery of his psychological centre. He says,

> For there is a psychological Center within us, a point where our personalities become connected to God . . . Joseph had found this Center. When his egocentricity was burned away on the journey to Egypt, he found his Center and began to live from it . . . All of this gave Joseph strength. He did not disintegrate in Pharaoh's dungeon; he did not become bitter, cynical or self-pitying. With this attitude it was only a matter of time until he became as free on the outside as he was on the inside.[10]

And so the story is really about us and comes to us from deep within our beings. That is why it resonates with us so richly. This story is part of our interior being, but one which has been hidden from us by our inattention to the reality we are. It lies deep within and has to be drawn out of us. We have been distracted from it by the illusions of contemporary existence. We have been prevented from reading it in depth by a false attention to the origins of the text or the complexities of authorship or by a need to prove that it is literally true. We then have to own the story as ours and stand within it and accept that it is about us. When this happens the path to our own redemption becomes clear.

The German writer, Thomas Mann, rewrote the Joseph

[10]Ibid., p. 65.

story in his epic work *Joseph and His Brothers*. This is a
lengthy retelling of the story populated by the characters we
find in the biblical narrative but also by a whole crowd of
others from Mann's imagination. It is a rich story set in the
depths of the human consciousness. In it the biblical characters sometimes merge with those of Greek mythology. Esau,
for example, Jacob's brother, at one point becomes Pan,
playing the pipes with pointed ears, explicitly described as
'a musical goat'. The man Joseph meets in the field whom
he asks 'Where are my brothers?' is a form of Hermes, the
guide of travellers. These devices are used by Mann not
because he thinks a dull story must be brightened up for
modern readers, but in order to root the story deep within
our consciousness as human beings. He wants to show that
it is not just from one part of the past but from all of our
pasts. It is not simply one story like any other but a story
which roots the reader in the stream of human consciousness,
places her or him in the middle of a pattern of life which
comes to us all from what he calls 'the deep well of the
past'. He is saying, as it were, 'This is the pattern of things.
This is how it was with Moses, with Jacob, with Joseph.
This is how it was with Jesus. This, too, is how it is with
us. We all have to go through the same pattern.' 'Even,' he
is saying, 'even the classical gods are part of the same basic
pattern of things. They do not escape it either, and so they
can appear in the same story.' As we have seen, this is a
very Jungian point of view. While he was writing the book
Mann said, 'What I should like to express is the transformation of Tradition into Present as timeless mystery, or the
experiencing of the self as myth.' It is precisely this 'transformation of Tradition into Present' that we miss so often
when we read the Bible. It is not so much a question of
believing whether the story happened or not just like it says,
nor a question of finding the various sources of this or that
part of the text. We are not being asked to understand the
text or even to believe the text. We are being asked *to become*
the text. That is what Mann does with his magnificent
retelling of the Joseph story. He shows us how we, with all

of our mental and intellectual luggage, with all of our twenti-
eth-century sophistication, can belong to this story.

Many people will find this shocking because of the liberties
it takes with the text of Scripture. We cannot, they will say,
re-invent or re-imagine the past, particularly the past as it
has been given to us in this book. It is, after all, a sacred
text. But before we protest too much it is worth thinking a
little about this sacred text and to see how it works in itself.
We should remember that the Joseph story cannot, in spite
of the efforts of all the historians, be linked to any one period
in Egyptian history. Parts of it relate to an earlier period when
marriage by Egyptians to foreigners was tolerated, others to
another, later period. It is not history. Rather it is a 'myth'
invented and told by the story-teller – that great pastor of
souls – to enable people to understand themselves more
clearly. The final editor has woven together elements from a
number of earlier narratives in order to do this. Whether the
final editor was the court historian envisaged by one scholar
or the woman writer dreamed up by another, the point is
that they were doing this at the time of Solomon, writing
midrash as it is called, in order to enable the people around
them to have a coherent pattern of understanding of what
was happening to them at that time. This is just what Thomas
Mann does in *Joseph and His Brothers*. He does, as far as we
can see, more or less exactly what the biblical writers themselves were doing. He merely has the disadvantage of writing
so many thousands of years after the last biblical editor of
the story, but his method and purpose are very much the
same. The biblical writers gathered the story together to give
coherence and understanding to the people of their day, to
give them a myth by which to understand themselves in the
crises they were facing. Mann does the same. Obviously there
are differences, sometimes quite fundamental, between
Thomas Mann's handling of the story and that of the final
editor of Genesis 37–50, but they are not so very far apart in
their intentions. They both intend to tell the story in such a
way as to provide a narrative within which human beings
can find meaning for their lives.

The interesting thing is that Mann began *Joseph and His*

Brothers during the rise of Hitler and completed it in America where he had taken refuge from Nazism. Writing it helped him bear his exile from Germany and the knowledge of Hitler's attempt to exterminate the Jewish people. He wrote it to assuage his own grief but also to provide a context for the grief and tragedy of others. But this should not really surprise us, for the Joseph story has just that quality. It is a story which helps people put tragedy into context. The attempted genocide of the Jews is a case in point. The Joseph story has frequently been used by Jewish commentators since Auschwitz, seen by them as some sort of commentary on the Holocaust. The cistern, or slavery, or Egypt, is the place of destruction where the dreamers in our society, the creative ones blessed with the knowledge of God, have to go. In his book of essays about reconciliation in Europe, Rabbi Albert Friedlander retells the story of the occasion when he was asked to lecture to Protestant students at the Kirchliche Hochschule in Wuppertal. He took the opportunity to comment on the text from the Joseph story which reads, 'Here comes this dreamer. Come now, let us kill him and throw him into one of the pits . . .'[11] Friedlander says, 'We know the story. But what would this text sound like if we translated it into the language of the twentieth century? *achad ha-borot*, "one of the cisterns". Why not "some dark valley called Babi Yar"? Why not "a gas oven"? That is how people dealt with one another, even yesterday.'[12] He sees the direct parallel, as have others, between Joseph's descent into potential death and slavery and the descent of the Jews into the Holocaust. He says, 'Joseph does not die, although he undertakes the journey into the underworld of the slaves and so experiences something of death.'[13] The interesting thing about Friedlander's exposition is that he points out that Joseph is reconciled to his brothers, something which holds out hope for reconciliation between Jews and Christians. He says, '. . . we must

[11]Genesis 37:19–20, 'pits' is sometimes translated 'cisterns'.
[12]Albert Friedlander, *A Thread of Gold – Journeys towards Reconciliation* (SCM Press 1989), p. 32.
[13]Ibid., p. 33.

visit the darkest valleys of our landscape, and we must then find the way back.'[14]

And so not just for Christians, who look for models of redemption in the Hebrew Bible and find them more often sometimes than the text justifies, but also for contemporary Jews, the Joseph story is about ourselves and our need for reconciliation and forgiveness. It is so because the writer, or at least the final editor, has allowed his imagination to work within the material he has received to make it into something of a comment, what Jews call a *midrash*, on his circumstances. This enables us to do the same in each generation, so that instead of dying with the writer the text lives again and again. To use again the analogy of the Bible as an old family photograph album, this photograph, or set of photographs, of the people of God as represented by Joseph and his descent into Egypt, is one of those to which we return most frequently. When we come to these pages we find that they are thumbed and dirtied by use. The photographs are marked with finger-prints and the stains of coffee cups left by people poring over them so often. And these fingerprints are not just from our immediate family either, but from others whom we do not always know or trust very well, people from other communities who we do not believe can have the same interest in our family history. But all people come to look at these pictures. They are common property. Here we can see our own like-nesses almost more than anywhere else. Here we can see that we all look like Joseph. We were there too. And we are all his brothers and sisters. Each generation of his sisters and brothers has to go back and find this place, remake this descent into the pit and retrace the pattern of his life. We all have to mark the photographs with our own prints and so rediscover our identity, our capacity for compassion in the face of adversity, and so come home together.

[14]Ibid.

7

'A Space Within Which God Can Act'
(Matthew 5:1–12)

Each of us has our own way of understanding the Sermon on the Mount and in particular its opening section, the Beatitudes (Matthew 5:1–12). These sayings of Jesus have been words of hope and encouragement for countless numbers of people in the past. They speak to many in our own day of the way in which the poor and the downtrodden will one day find happiness. They are words of promise in a difficult world, but above all they are words of promise to 'the little people' who have little to hope for and little to live for.

Recent New Testament scholarship has supported this way of looking at the Beatitudes. Modern scholars have been struck by the totally paradoxical nature of these sayings. Why should the poor be blessed? Why should those who mourn be comforted? But a look at the way in which the Scriptures use language shows that the use of such paradoxes is not new to Jesus or the New Testament, but one of the language patterns the Bible uses when speaking of the way God acts. In the Psalms, for example, it is said that God, the Holy One of Israel, lifts up those who are on the dungheap. In a number of places these paradoxical patterns are used to show how God elevates those who are normally regarded as beyond help. They ask us to see God as being the one who comes close to those whom, in everyday life, we would regard as being far from God. So the Beatitudes are not new or different, they simply focus for us the paradoxical way in which the Scriptures are forced to speak about the activity of God if they are to speak truly. God is both the Holy One who is utterly beyond all that we know, and also the One who comes down into the very depths of the creation to make his nature known.

Modern scholarship has also been caught up in exploring what is known as the eschatological nature of the Bible. The Bible is always looking forward to what is to come. The Beatitudes are no exception. They anticipate what is to come, saying it is present now. The glory that will be is available now. What is normally regarded as appertaining to the coming age of the Messiah is said to be present in this age. Once again this is a familiar pattern of speech in the Scriptures, marking the way in which the believer has this deep sense of living in overlapping worlds. God not only summons us to live in hope but also gives us a foretaste of that hope. We look forward, but, for those who believe, what is in the future is already present now.

The third thing that contemporary scholarship about the Beatitudes tells us is that the two different versions of them, in Matthew and Luke, reveal something about the life of the Church and how it accommodates the word which God speaks to it. Even within the short space of time between the two Gospels there is evidence of a movement away from the intense, abrupt and uncompromising form in which Jesus first spoke these words. The form of the Beatitudes is not the same in Matthew as it is in Luke. The subtle shifts of emphasis from the way the Beatitudes are set down in Luke's Gospel – probably the earlier form – compared to the form of words found in Matthew, illustrate how these words have been used in the life of the church, and their meaning and form subtly changed. The development shows that people found the original stark message of Jesus hard to take. There was, therefore, a process of assimilation whereby the stark, original message is related to the human capacities of its hearers and balanced against the demands of everyday life. In this way 'Blessed are you who are poor' (Luke), becomes 'Blessed are the poor in spirit' (Matthew). There is a tension, an inevitable and necessary tension, between the requirements of everyday existence and the constantly renewed demands of Jesus' teaching. Each generation has to hear these words afresh and take them into themselves in a new way. This does not detract from the truth of the Scriptures, it simply shows how the word of God is something which is being continually spoken within the creation and how at every turn of the road we have to listen for and hear this word. If we are deaf, we might even stumble across it without expecting to do so.

It is this which fascinates me most. The word of the Beatitudes is hidden just beneath the surface of our existence. Every now and again it seems to surface. Somebody stumbles across its presence and importance and decides to live the Beatitudes in his or her life. The obvious example of this in the life of the Church is St Francis of Assisi. He found the simplicity and joy of the Beatitudes and devoted himself to living that way. It meant a definitive break with the life of a young Italian nobleman and the desires of his father, but it made an infinite difference not just to him but to countless numbers of people since. The same can occur in our own generation and I want to use this chapter trying to illustrate how the Beatitudes have, as it were, been 'found' by different people in different circumstances. The word of the Beatitudes is not dead.

Allow me to start with my own life. I have a particular affection for the Beatitudes because they were very much involved in my decision to be a priest. And the Beatitudes have cropped up, as it were, in my life on a very regular basis ever since. They seem to be never very far away and every now and again emerge from my consciousness to recall and restore me to my proper self.

The story of how this happened could be anyone's story and most probably is shared by others who have grown through the same period of history and thought that I have. The reason for telling it is because it illustrates how our inner lives and the words of the Scriptures are at root the same. If we are patient enough with ourselves and give enough time and attention to our experience and look within our depths we shall, I believe, find within us the biblical patterns of which I have spoken. We shall find, hidden deep within us, the word God utters which gives life to all humankind. But this journey to the hidden word of life is a very slow one and requires much patience and a great deal of inner silence and attention to God. And it always involves hindsight as well as perceptiveness about what is happening to us now. When we look back on our lives we find that God has spoken his word within us. My intention in sharing my experience of the Beatitudes is to encourage others to look deep within themselves and to realise that what appears to be drab and uninspiring, far removed from the wonderful lives led by the saints and the glamourous people we read about, is in fact full of the bread of God's word.

I came to realise the importance of the Beatitudes for myself when I was an undergraduate. I was a student of French Language and Literature. I enjoyed my work and during my final year spent some time debating the rival claims of being a teacher or a diplomat when I left the university. My ideas of where I would be going after graduation were fairly romantic and cloudy. It was also true that I was a devout, if not pious, young man and a Bible group leader in the student chaplaincy. People had wondered whether I might not be ordained.

During my final year I found it very difficult to decide what I should do next. In the end I gave up thinking about it and occupied myself with trying to pass my final examinations. But immediately these were over I turned away from French literature to read a number of the books which I had determined to read as soon as I had the time. Everybody then was talking about Dietrich Bonhoeffer and I plunged myself into his book, *The Cost of Discipleship*.

As is now well known Dietrich Bonhoeffer was one of the leaders of what was called 'The Confessing Church' in Germany before the war. The Confessing Church was that part of the German Lutheran Church which opposed the Hitler regime and in particular the insistence of the Nazis that the Civil Service and the Church should not appoint to positions of authority any person who had non-aryan (i.e. Jewish) ancestry. In protest against this Bonhoeffer and a number of others, including Pastor Niemöller, formed the Emergency League of Pastors which eventually became the Confessing Church. This breakaway Church asked Bonhoeffer to lead their seminary in the Black Forest for the training of pastors and it was there that Bonhoeffer wrote, among other things, *The Cost of Discipleship*. As one of Bonhoeffer's biographers says, the book is '. . . hard-lived, hard-prayed for stuff' which '. . . explores what it means to be a disciple. What is God demanding of us? What does it mean to follow Christ?'[1] The whole thing gripped me. I remember reading the book with great intensity. I even bought a copy for a member of my discussion group when he finished his examinations.

Looking back on the book now, thirty years later, much of it is dated or has been shown to be very one-sided, coloured by the circumstances in which it was written; but then it was extremely powerful. The main section of the book is an exposition of the Sermon on the Mount (Matthew 5–7). It begins, however, with a call for the church to accept a life of costly rather than cheap grace. Bonhoeffer says,

> Costly grace is the treasure hidden in the field; for the sake of it a man will gladly go and sell all that he has. It is the pearl of great price to buy which the merchant will sell all his goods. It is the kingly rule of Christ, for whose sake a man will pluck out the eye which causes him to stumble, it is the call of Jesus Christ at which the disciple leaves his nets and follows him.[2]

After that uncompromising opening Bonhoeffer moves on to an exposition of the Beatitudes (Matthew 5:1–12). For him these sayings are addressed particularly to the disciples, to those who have responded to the call of Jesus to follow him. The disciples are those who have renounced everything but now have everything with and through God. They are, consequently, 'blessed'. They have obeyed the call of Jesus. And each one of the Beatitudes is understood in this light.

> *Blessed are the poor in spirit* . . . They are poor because they have lost all in the following. They are '. . . the little band who for the sake of Jesus live a life of absolute renunciation and poverty.'

[1]Mary Bosanquet, *The Life and Death of Dietrich Bonhoeffer* (Hodder and Stoughton 1968), p. 187.
[2]Dietrich Bonhoeffer, *The Cost of Discipleship* (SCM 1959), p. 36.

Blessed are they that mourn . . . They are those who do without what the world means by peace and prosperity. 'The world dreams of progress, of power and of the future, but the disciples meditate on the end, the last judgement and the coming of the kingdom'. They are 'strangers in the world, unwelcome guests and disturbers of the peace.'

Blessed are the meek . . . These are those who are powerless and disenfranchised and who do not wield power.[3]

And so it goes on, through each one of the verses. The blessed are those who have renounced their rights, those who have renounced their own righteousness and who stand with Jesus in the shadow of the cross. This distinguishes them from the world and for this the world will reject them. The Fellowship of the Beatitudes is directly described as the Fellowship of the Crucified.

Clearly there is a great deal in Bonhoeffer's way of looking at the Beatitudes which is too stark and demanding. It is too obviously written by someone who is engaged in training pastors for the ministry in a very critical situation. The seminary at Finkenwalde was being investigated by the Gestapo and was eventually closed down. The pastors themselves were at grave risk because they would not accept the racial requirements of the Nazi state. They were looking once again to the roots of their theology and beginning to question the received Lutheran tradition about the links between church and state. Many were arrested. Bonhoeffer himself was eventually hung. It is small wonder that the Beatitudes were expounded in terms of the crucifixion.

But this exposition was also a proper reaction against the moralising of so much of the traditional teaching at the time. It had become clear to Bonhoeffer that much of what passed for Christianity was a form of moralism, no more than the best way of leading a good life. An exposition of Christianity which placed at its centre the death and resurrection of Jesus Christ and radical discipleship in his name and a life

[3]Ibid., p. 95ff.

commitment to his particular way, however familiar now, was at that time very disturbing and held in deep suspicion by traditional churchgoers. It was also clear to Bonhoeffer that this traditional, moralistic way of understanding Christianity which he inherited had failed, for so many of those who were devoted to the best way of leading a good life were now selling themselves to a manifestly evil state. There seemed to be nothing within their reading of the faith which could stop them from accepting what was required of them by the Nazis, including the controversial 'Aryan Paragraph' which required the Church to reject those of non-aryan ancestry when making appointments. This was clearly not good enough and so the liberal, idealist tradition of the Lutheran Church in which Bonhoeffer was brought up had to be replaced with something a great deal more radical. For him the call of Christ was not simply a call to good behaviour or true morality. It was not just the moral way – as it was, say, for Gandhi, in his exposition of the Sermon on the Mount. It was, rather, an absolute demand which brought the disciple before the face of the living God and into conflict with the powers of this world and so into the fellowship of the cross. This was the final freedom. A commitment to live out this call was the only proper foundation for morality. The following of a moral way was, Bonhoeffer would argue, in itself no guarantee that the call had been heard or that a full response had been made.[4]

I read all this with a sense that my own way was now open and not long afterwards offered myself for ordination. It was a step into unknown territory – indeed it was the first step into a lifetime commitment of moving forwards into unknown territory, a lifetime of trying to live in total openness to God – God in myself, God in other people, as well as God in the future and in the gift of life each day. All that I learned subsequently. At that time I was called by the challenge of the Beatitudes. What that challenge would contain was to be worked out over a lifetime.

I felt I had stumbled across something which seemed to be

[4]A very powerful recent exposition of this point is made by Nicholas Peter Harvey in *The Morals of Jesus* (DLT 1991).

embedded deep within my consciousness and which had been embedded there from the beginning. What was there was part of the way things truly were and had to be accepted and allowed to grow and flourish in my life if this life was to be lived fully and lived as before and with God. The Beatitudes were not just something in the New Testament but something in me.

Things did not stop there either, for this was not the last time that I would encounter the Beatitudes in this way. Some years after ordination I found myself working with students. At several points during the time that I was engaged in that ministry – which lasted over a considerable period of time and happened in a number of different places – the Beatitudes again became a touchstone for discipleship. One of them came through my visits to the Community of Taizé. The Taizé Community is a modern, ecumenical, monastic community in Burgundy which each year attracts thousands of young people to share in its worship and to listen to the expositions of Scripture given by the brothers. I had known Taizé since 1964 when my wife and I led the English delegation to a young person's workcamp nearby and visited the community with our French friends. I was entranced by the place from that moment, for here on the top of a hill a small group of brothers had gathered to work for reconciliation and unity. Their life was simple but dedicated and they were also so obviously in love with the beauty of things – the beauty of music in worship, the beauty of the surrounding countryside, and the beauty of life itself which in Europe had been so disfigured by war and then the Cold War since. I found the Rule of Taizé and read it. It contained so much of what Christianity meant for me and opened new ways for my exploring. So it was not surprising that soon after I began my work with students I took a group of them to Taizé. Before we went I talked with them about the place and shared with them something of the rule of the community and the way of life which they had developed. Brother Roger, the prior and founder of Taizé, had written this rule in the very early days of the community. At first he had resisted attempts to persuade him that the community should have a rule, arguing that this could lead to a degree of institutionalisation which would be harmful and which had proved harmful to other, older monastic traditions. In the end, during a long retreat in the winter of 1952–3, Brother Roger wrote the Rule of Taizé which now forms the basis of their common life.

But this rule is not like any other. It does not contain explicit instructions about the routines of daily living. It is more a lyrical expression of the ideals which the Gospels set for those who wish to live together in a common brotherhood. Indeed, it bears a closer resemblance to the early rule drawn up by St Francis for his 'poor brothers' than to any of the major monastic rules of Christian history. St Francis' early rule was very close to the Gospels. Brother Roger's rule is the same. The central section is entitled, 'Be Filled With The Spirit Of The Beatitudes: Joy, Mercy, Simplicity'. He deliberately recalls his brothers to a life lived according to the blessedness announced by Jesus at the beginning of the Sermon on the Mount. The interesting and arresting thing about Brother Roger's exposition of the Beatitudes – and here he differs from Dietrich Bonhoeffer – is that whereas the Beatitudes in Matthew are eight or nine in number, Brother Roger concentrates them into three – joy, mercy and simplicity. Of these three only mercy is specifically mentioned in the actual text in Matthew's Gospel. Joy and simplicity are not explicitly mentioned. Far from being a desecration of the text such a move is a stroke of genius and actually does no more than what the Church has always done with its sacred texts – re-expresses them in a way which speaks to the age and which conveys to that age the inner meaning of the words, a process which can be found at work even within the text of Scripture itself. For those three attributes – joy, simplicity and mercy – do actually seem to encapsulate so much of what Jesus was saying. A few quotations from Brother Roger's rule will illustrate this.

> Perfect joy is self-giving. Whoever knows it seeks neither gratitude nor kindness. It is sheer wonder renewed by the sight of the generosity of the Giver of all gifts . . .

> Anyone who lives in mercy is neither over-sensitive nor

constantly disappointed. He gives himself simply, forgetting himself; joyfully, with all his heart, freely, not looking for anything in return . . .

Availability means constantly simplifying your mode of living . . . Simplicity is also loyalty towards oneself as a way of acquiring limpidity. It is a way of openness towards our neighbour . . .

Simplicity lies in the free joy of a brother who has given up any obsession with his own progress or backsliding to keep his eyes fixed on the light of Christ . . .[5]

However different from the actual words of the Beatitudes in the New Testament this is so very near to their inner spirit.

I came away from Taizé that time even more determined to try to live in the spirit expressed by those words. But the story does not end there. Some years later I went back, again with a group of students on an ecumenical pilgrimage. On this visit I had elected to spend the whole week there in silence. I wanted to use the time reading and meditating on the meaning of the Beatitudes. It was a week which I have since realised was of immense importance in my life. It represented a very deep inner renewal of my faith. I still have the notes I made during the retreat, written in tiny writing on scraps of paper and headed with the name of each day. I have them with me now and they bring back rich memories of that summer. We had decided to go from England by minibus and to take tents so that we could camp on the way down and back as well as be fairly independent while we were there. I bought a small two-man tent for the occasion. It was a hot summer and hardly rained the whole ten days we were away. My notes are full of evocative hints of the quality and depth of the whole pilgrimage. They begin,

Long journey the first day with some mistakes but beautiful stopping places – pools of rest – in a lane in Normandy, by a river and lake S. of Paris and then, eventually, by the

[5]Brother Roger of Taizé, *A Parable of Community – Basic Texts from the Taizé Community* (Les Presses de Taizé 1980), p. 244.

river in Autun. An evening exploration of Autun took us
to the Cathedral and we came upon the glorious tympanum
by Giselbertus over the west door – Christ in majesty . . .
on to Taizé where after some misdirection found the silent
field and put up tent. Music in church so beautiful. Resonates deep within me . . .

I had brought a book about the Beatitudes to use during the
week. Reading this book,[6] reflecting on the Beatitudes, resting
in silence, walking through the Burgundy countryside, sharing in the beauty of the prayer in the church, all this marked
a sort of turning-point for me. I don't think much happened
immediately, or even very soon afterwards, but the seeds had
been sown. What was sown was a sense of abandonment into
God, a sort of relinquishing of self and glad acceptance that
God is, that he is in us and in all things, that all will be well.
This is reflected in the notes I made and the quotations I
noted down as important.

> The Beatitudes draw for us a very strange picture of the
> man who is blessed. He is poor and unimpressive, hungry
> and in mourning, trodden on and yet able to make
> peace . . .

> Blessed are the poor in spirit, those who have allowed
> themselves to be stripped of the old spirit, the spirit of
> acquisitiveness and 'security' for theirs is the Kingdom of
> Heaven, because they no longer seek to possess but to be
> possessed, to lose themselves and theirs is the ecstasy of
> simple receiving and giving again . . .

> No amount of trying ever produced the desired result . . .
> the accomplishment always has the quality of a surprise, a
> gift, an accident . . .

> God's world is pleroma. Our world is deficiency, hyster-
> oma. God acts from the fullness of his being. We must
> abandon the kind of activism which belongs to hysteroma
> to live rather by the unobtrusiveness of God . . .

[6]Simon Tugwell OP, *Reflections on the Beatitudes* (DLT 1980).

We must learn to be incomplete, a space within which God can act . . .

There is a mystery at the source of ourselves. Purity of heart enables us to look at things again and enjoy them . . .

If you are worried nothing is gained by trying to get rid of the worry . . .[7]

In order to live I had to *be* the Beatitudes. I had to open myself and live my ministry in simplicity, mercy and joy, leaving so much more to God than I had ever done or, if truth be known, had ever thought of doing. I had to abandon the view that it was always or only the Church which could correct and heal and to allow the Church to be God's, and allow his action to move through me and, blessed relief, *for* me. I was much further on than when I had read Bonhoeffer as a student years ago, but once again the Beatitudes had spoken. Whereas before they had spoken in challenge and in summons, now it was a call to delight.

On the Friday of the week at Taizé my notes record how Brother Roger and his brothers brought the icon of the cross into the church and laid it in the centre, illuminated by two lamps. People came around it to pray and lay down their burdens.

Did this, with old evangelical hymns echoing through my head – and offered self and all my/our brokenness, failures etc., to his safe keeping. Slept.

The next day was the Feast of St Thomas and the Gospel reading speaks about Thomas putting his hand into the side of Christ, '. . . do not doubt, but believe'. I knew that this was what I had to do and my notes end with the need to put my hand into the side of Christ.

Since that time I have known that the Beatitudes are what I come home to. They are at the root of my faith and when I come to their reality I am refreshed and reconstituted. I

[7]Ibid.

have attempted to convey this significance in Bible study sessions and sermons.

The interesting part of it all, in reflection, is how the Beatitudes continue to speak to us today. They spoke to me, but they have also spoken to the society of which I am a part. I found it so fascinating that in the face of persecution Bonhoeffer had found his inspiration in these words and had encouraged his fledgling pastors with his exposition of their significance. Nazism destroyed a great deal, but it failed to eradicate the living presence of those words in the hearts and minds of the Church. Eventually Nazism had tripped over the words 'Blessed are you who are poor . . .'. The same dramatic movement was being worked out, I felt, in the Taizé community. Brother Roger had come to Taizé and attempted to live some of these things out in reality. He had assisted Jewish refugees fleeing from Nazism. He had lived simply. He had found joy in brotherhood and in the praise of God. His community reflected that and bore his words about mercy, simplicity and joy at their heart. And as they did this they found themselves overwhelmed by the young people of Europe and beyond. It was almost as if these young people, affluent, well educated, articulate, had subconsciously and very tentatively, come to the realisation that they were living a dream and, seeing Taizé, found themselves stumbling on the reality of life, tripping over the presence of God deep within their existence. Kneeling with them in the great Church of Reconciliation in Taizé, singing the prayer with them, you can see it, you can feel it within yourself, as one by one, slowly and hesitantly, they stand up and make their way across the church to talk to a brother. You can see it as they sit in groups around an exposition of Scripture with their heads on one side, thinking, wondering. It is as if the Beatitudes are a word hidden deep within us and deep within our collective existence that every so often we can, if we are open, find and live by. The circumstances of this openness and this 'finding' vary and cannot be predicted, but they do seem to be something to do with abandonment and openness. Bonhoeffer knew that he could not resist being with his people as war broke out and he returned to Germany from America to see, with enormous

pain, but also with open eyes, just what God's word was for
them all at that time. Roger Schultz, the founder of Taizé,
abandoned himself to the quest for brotherhood. As Simon
Tugwell says in the book I used, 'We must learn to be incomplete, a space within which God can act . . .'

At this point in my reflections I felt that I had come to
understand the Beatitudes in a particular way. They were
words in Scripture but they were also *a word* hidden deep
within our consciousness. For me the principal word was
simplicity, living without grasping, in total acceptance of all
life and all people as gift, a gift from God. Every now and
then, through a particular set of circumstances, human beings
become open to or aware of this word and as a consequence
some people – such as Bonhoeffer and Brother Roger – are
able then to live the Beatitudes with a particular force and
freshness. At this point I also became aware that looking at
things in this way, seeing the text of Scripture more as a
symbol or catalyst for living in a particular way, as *a word*
which produced life rather than words to be believed or examined, was not the usual way of looking at things. I was saying,
it seemed, that the words of Scripture were not prescriptive,
or at least not prescriptive in that old sense of telling us what
to do, something like recipes for action or words from the
past which should be followed now. Instead they were words
which were effective symbols of what could happen, sacra-
ments of the activity of God hidden deep within things. In a
real sense the Scriptures were us and what they were talking
about was not something we ought to do if we were strong
or good enough, although that came into it, but rather they
were talking about what could happen, what had, in a sense,
always happened within us if only we would allow it to surface
and become part of our everyday reality.

The question then became whether this way of looking at
things was acceptable. It was, as I said, not the normal way
of looking at Scripture. So I had to ask myself, 'what does
contemporary scholarship about the Beatitudes say?' I then
remembered all that about the shifts between St Luke's version of the Beatitudes and St Matthew's. I was somewhat
relieved. I was relieved because it showed, if nothing else,

how the reception and recording of these words at the time of their utterance demonstrates the same or similar patterns as their reception by those who hear them now. Bonhoeffer heard the uncompromising words of Jesus but had to bring them into relationship with the circumstances of his day. Brother Roger had done the same. We assimilate them into our complexities, we balance them against the demands of our lives as the Apostles and Evangelists did then and just as the Church has always done. For the Beatitudes are not – and indeed this applies to any other part of Scripture – a set of injunctions, not an unchanging blueprint. This at least should be clear from the differences which exist between the two versions in Matthew and Luke. But the fact that this is so does not diminish their authority, rather it enhances it. It turns the authority of the Beatitudes into a living authority rather than a literal one. We are called to *be* people of the Beatitudes and allow the power and relevance of the blessedness of which they speak to transform our lives in each generation. How it will be for each of us will be different at different times in our lives. How it will be for the church will be different according to the situation in which the church finds itself. We are not called to the same type or style of Beatitude in this generation as Bonhoeffer was in his. We may, at another point in history, be called to live a form of Beatitude which may be less, but may be even more stringent than his was. We need above all to keep awake to the action of God.

This is why, in Brother Roger's treatment of the Beatitudes in the Rule of Taizé, he reduces the Beatitudes to three – joy, mercy and simplicity. For him these attributes effect the radical openness of the soul to God that the Beatitudes of Jesus demand. Throughout the Rule there is a constant emphasis on openness and transparency.

> Open yourself to all that is human . . .
> In the transparency of brotherly love . . .
> Simplicity is . . . a way of openness towards our
> neighbour . . .

This openness then prepares and enables the soul to take the risk of living the Beatitudes each day and each moment of each day. It will enable the brother to take the great step of living in true community and risking his all in brotherly love. It will enable him to live first of all with Christ and then with the poor when the call comes to do that and then to live with the rich when the call comes to do that. One of the things Brother Roger has come to know well and often writes about in his journals is the way in which modern living precludes the way of openness. Modern living has become a way of acquisition not openness, a way which leads to a hardening of the heart and a closing of the way to God. This is why the Beatitudes are so forceful, they break open the carapace of modern acquisitive living.

So the Beatitudes are not an exact set of words which we must follow. They are symbols of the truth which lives within us and towards which we must open ourselves. Perhaps they are best compared to the tip of an iceberg. The words we hear or read are what we see of the iceberg, but the greater part of the iceberg remains hidden. What its shape is we cannot always tell until we look and see. It will certainly turn out to be bigger and more mysterious than we thought when we first saw the words on the page. The words are signals of a greater word, a hidden reality, the hidden word within ourselves and within our existence, within the existence of the created universe, which is Christ, the hidden word of God. It is his reality which will call us and by which we must live. Once we do this then different things will happen in different situations. The Beatitudes can be taken in a political sense – as a statement that those who are persecuted are those who contain within them the presence and message of God. We, in our turn, if we are to be 'with' God, must join them in no uncertain fashion, and there are those who are following that way. But the Beatitudes can also be taken in a deeply personal sense, as a personal challenge to live in openness and simplicity. They can be a challenge to action or a challenge to live in praise and deep acceptance of what has been given. This second way is less visible, almost invisible. It is probably the way most people follow. This secret way is no less honourable, no less grace filled, indeed, no less 'charismatic' than the more visible way. At different times in history the

Beatitudes have been all these things and many more. How they will impinge upon us in the future we cannot know.

The point is that we must always be ready for the hidden part of the iceberg, always prepared for the hidden reality of God, always open to the hidden word and what it has to say to us and call us to do. The extreme paradoxes of the Beatitudes and their radically eschatological nature are ways of signalling this to us. Their very paradoxicality is intended to keep us open to possibilities of which we know nothing. Their eschatological tenour is meant to force us to keep our eyes open to further horizons as yet unrevealed. What we need to see is at present kept from us. Reading and hearing the Beatitudes is the way Christ gives us of keeping us open to the possibilities of God.

One of the most important things I have come to see through reflecting upon the place of the Beatitudes in modern life is that the Christian discipline of prayer and the sacramental life, the regular praise and hearing of the word of God, is the *normal* means by which the openness and simplicity of which the Beatitudes speak is preserved for and within the believer. This is how we become a space within which God can act. If we pray in an open spirit regularly and praise God in the sacramental life then we will be ready to hear the word of the Beatitudes when it comes. The effect on me of those days at Taizé (and, I must say, at one or two other places since then) has been to simplify my prayer, to enable me to pray in deeper confidence, knowing that the Spirit prays within me. I value the opportunity to come to prayer in openness, just as I am. On my way to chapel in the mornings I have ceased, usually, to play the car radio, preferring silence or music so that my spirit can be ready for the word. I try to come to the Eucharist, whether it is a full, solemn and crowded service or a small, silent one, with a spirit of total openness and attention, listening for the word of salvation and ready to receive the Christ into my life. I find it such a pity that the usual eucharistic experience for most Christians today is of a noisy one with lots of music. There is nothing wrong in this, and indeed, so much to give thanks for after the long period of formality that the Church has gone through, but I do long for people to be able to come to Christ in space and silence, so that this space and silence can challenge the noisiness of their daily lives, otherwise the Eucharist is simply an extension of that noise and gives them no chance to pay attention to the word which God has spoken within them from their beginnings. In conversation I try to be attentive to what it is that is being said to me by others in case this is a word from God. I listen to them and attempt – sadly not always successfully – to pay them the 'courtesy' that Christ pays them. I try to live in simplicity, not without possessions, but valuing the singularity of the possessions I have and giving where I can to those without and counting myself ready to abandon what I have, both in money and talents when it is called for. All of that discipline of the spirit is a daily struggle and I have to come back to it daily and make myself more ready for it by regular retreats and quiet days. But I know now that this is what living the Beatitudes means for me.

I also know only too well that this discipline can die, but my great confidence is that God continually speaks his word. And so when the spirit is weak and human co-operation in the work of God dies away God is still at work, uttering his word, giving us his bread. If we allow the carapace of modern acquisitive living to come between us and that word then occasionally it is broken open for us by other, extraordinary means.

God gives us the bread of his word always, but sometimes he gives it to us in strange ways and we may be forced to live the Beatitudes through means which we would not ordinarily choose. An enforced 'stripping' is one such means. A recent television documentary showed the effect that being taken hostage had had upon the lives of a number of people. They were all taken hostage in unexpected circumstances for considerable periods of time but all returned to modern living with their attitudes cleansed and their acquisitiveness purged. One returned to the Church and followed the mystical way, seeking silence and a simpler lifestyle, staying close to his family and friends after having been a somewhat hedonistic personality. Another revised his business life, another mended his breaking marriage. All began to live the Beatitudes. The television producer is said to have made the programme in a sceptical mood thinking that such people would be the exceptions amongst those taken hostage, but after interviewing a number of them, not all of whom eventually appeared on the programme, he was forced to admit that such changes were the general rule. The exceptions were those who were hardened or embittered by their experience.

God feeds us his bread always. He feeds it through Scripture and through the church which is the bearer of his word, but he also gives it all of the time to all of his children, some of whom come to find it in the midst of terrible suffering.

8

'I Will Only Tell You Once'

(Epistle to the Romans)

We don't always realise what the Epistle to the Romans is about. It is not, at least not in the first instance, a letter about how everybody is sinful or about how you and I are saved. It does talk about those things and it does tell Christians what Paul thinks salvation means. But all that is subordinate to the main purpose of the letter, which is to say who is part of God's people and why.

Paul held a controversial belief, one which was attacked from both sides during his lifetime. Gentiles, he believed, could become part of the people of God through their faith in Jesus Christ, without needing to accept all of the requirements of the Jewish Law. He held this belief, however, not because he wanted to be controversial, nor, as many people think, because he wanted to form a new people of God separate from the old one. On the contrary, he held this belief precisely because he wanted to keep the whole people of God together. He wanted the different parts to live in a constructive and fruitful fellowship and believed that what he was saying was the only way in which this could really happen. Other people's recipes were the divisive ones.

The key to understanding what Paul had to say is to realise that he lived, moved, and preached and spoke 'among Jews and Gentiles'. In other words his views were formed as a response to a situation in which both Jews, obviously and traditionally, but now also, it seemed, and that strangely and to many very frighteningly, Gentiles, were all God's people. Gentiles were being brought to faith in the God of Israel through their discipleship of Jesus the Christ. Could this really be so? If it was so, how could it be understood? What did this make of God's covenant with the Jewish people? And above all what did it make of God? What was God up to? Had he changed his mind? Was his plan for all things still the same? Was there no consistency in the universe?

In all the fears and conflicting claims which were to be found in the church, Paul had come to a simple and clear perspective. At least what he had to say began from a simple and clear perspective, even if it sometimes got complicated in the telling. For Paul the basic perspective was that Gentile converts were full and genuine heirs to the promises made by God to Israel. When they professed their faith, even though they were not of Jewish parentage, they became part of the same people of God with the same access to God and the same blessing from God. Abraham, Isaac and Jacob were their ancestors in the faith just as they were the ancestors of those who were Jews by descent. Paul believed that Gentile converts to the faith enjoyed the blessing of God because of their faith in Jesus Christ.

That was the start and finish of it all, and Paul had believed this from the time of his call from God on the road to Damascus. That event was not a conversion in the strict sense, even though that is what it is often called, but a call to be the apostle to the Gentiles. Paul believed that his mission was to the Gentiles. He believed that these were the last days before the end of time, 'the latter days' predicted in the Hebrew Scriptures, when the Gentiles would turn to God. His place in God's plan was to proclaim that truth and to usher in, as it were, the last act of the play. His calling was to be priest to the Gentiles. He was to make the offering of the Gentiles to God as predicted in Isaiah 2. These believers, provided they forsook idols, led a moral life and turned to the God of Israel, were to be accepted as they were, that is as Gentiles. They were not required to become Jews. If they were asked to be circumcised, the normal physical sign of becoming a Jew, then this, Paul felt, was a denial of the validity of God's promises to them.

At first Paul's position was accepted. Jewish believers in Jesus accepted Gentile believers on Paul's terms. There was some argument, which is recorded in Galatians 2, but Paul's view was accepted by the chief apostles in Jerusalem.[1] He was to be the agent of God's promises to the Gentiles in the latter days. But this situation did not last. Some time later argument once again arose as to whether Gentile converts should accept the whole of the Law. Paul argued that this was not needed because such believers were 'righteoused by faith'. God's requirement of Gentiles was acceptance of the God of Israel and of Jesus as the Saviour, and no more.

What Paul was arguing for, in effect, was the view that the transformation of the convert by God – what he calls 'being righteoused by faith' – brought the believer into the same condition as that reached by Jews by observance of the Law. This did not mean that the Law was no longer needed or that Jewish people who had faith in Jesus as the Saviour should no longer observe the Law. It simply meant that God was doing the same for the Gentile converts as he had always done for everybody else but without the need for the Law as the way to righteousness in this case.

It would probably help us to understand this a little better if we now had a look at what was going on in the churches when Paul wrote his epistle. A debate was taking place. The question was, 'How was God's plan to be understood in relation to those who were not Jewish when they came to faith in the God of Israel through Jesus?' When we know this is the context a number of puzzling features and longstanding controversies become much clearer. When Romans was written this argument had been going for some time. It had already generated the Epistle to the Galatians and is referred to extensively in the Acts of the Apostles. But there were two further elements in the debate which affected the immediate context of the Epistle to the Romans. The first of these was a further twist in the argument about the effect that following Paul's way would have if it became the norm for everybody. The second is the situation which had arisen in Rome itself.

Let's consider these in turn. What was the new twist in the argument? People had been saying that if Paul's way of doing

[1]Acts 15.

things became the norm then Gentile converts would not be moral enough. It was not enough, people argued, just to allow Gentiles to be converted to the faith and then let them get on with it. They needed something stronger if the church was to be sure that they would follow the way. As people would say today, they needed firm teaching. Above all, it was said, they needed the backbone of the Law. How could they be trusted to behave properly as followers of the God of Israel if they did not accept in its fullness the Law which God had given and which was required of all other believers? They needed commitment to a clear moral standard. If you let them go on without the Law then there would be immorality and backsliding. People would revert, it was claimed, to the immorality of their pagan days and would not be sufficiently moral. The Epistle to the Romans begins with Paul's response to this argument.

Meanwhile, in Rome, a number of things had been happening which made this debate and its outcome particularly important for the Christians there. We have to remember that Emperor Claudius expelled the Jews from Rome in about 49 CE. He is said by Suetonius to have done so because of 'Jews who insisted on rioting at the instigation of Chrestus'. Scholars usually say that this is because there were religious riots over the messiahship of Jesus such that the emperor simply decided to get rid of all of the Jews. The incident is referred to in Acts 18:2. There is no evidence about how thorough or how long this ban on the Jews was, but scholars believe that Paul was writing to a church which because of this ban had inevitably become very much a Gentile church. Now, however, with the return of Jewish Christians the church had to resolve a number of questions which had remained unresolved for some years. How did these two groups relate? Why had all these Gentiles got so far? In the interval attitudes would have hardened and the dialogue had become more difficult. Should the Christian movement still remain, as it had been prior to the ban, within Judaism and so live Jewishly, or should it now be asked to carry on as a new and totally independent reality? Final separation was probably inevitable, but the situation Paul is addressing lies at some point before the separation but after the return of the Jewish Christians.

You can see how the Roman situation was one which affected Paul's theology in a particular way. He believed that he had the answer to the situation which they faced. He could resolve the conflict, even though he had not yet been to Rome, because he had faced it elsewhere. Hence his letter. What is interesting and important is that Paul seems to have taken a middle way. He believed very strongly that the church could not live independently of its Jewish roots. Christians had Abraham, Isaac and Jacob as their ancestors and worshipped, through Jesus, the God who gave the Torah to Moses. Paul makes it quite clear that God has not changed his mind. The old promises are still valid and God's pattern of action is totally consistent. The point is that Paul believed that Gentile Christians were taking the way that God had willed for the Gentiles all along. They had, as it were, discovered another meaning of the way which God had always proclaimed. Faith in Christ is the crucial matter for Gentiles. What faith in Christ brings is not new in the sense of being different, it is only new in the sense of bringing to the forefront what God's purposes for the Gentiles had been.

And so Paul is writing to the Christians in Rome in the same spirit that he writes all of his letters, that is to address a particular situation in a particular place. One or two modern scholars have helpfully compared the situation in Rome to that of Anglicans and Methodists in eighteenth- and nineteenth-century Britain.[2] Here too there was an overlapping situation between two groups of Christians which held for a while but which, in the end, did not last. Just as Christianity had sprung up within Judaism so Methodism had sprung up within the Anglican Church. Right through the nineteenth century many Methodists remained devout Anglicans. Following the example and teaching of their founder, they received communion at their parish church regularly in the morning, but worshipped as Methodists later in the day.

[2]Esp. Morna Hooker, cited in John Ziesler, *Paul's Letter to the Romans* (SCM New Testament Commentaries 1991), p. 14.

Others had come into the Methodist fellowship directly, without having been Anglicans in the first place and so did not feel the need to go to communion at an Anglican church. What they had within the Methodist fellowship was quite sufficient. In this situation, although he remained an Anglican until his death – just as Paul remained a Jew – John Wesley felt it necessary to ordain ministers to celebrate the Eucharist within the Methodist fellowship and so sow the seeds of final separation. The parallels with the situation behind the Epistle to the Romans are not exact, but the circumstances must have felt very similar to Paul and John Wesley as they struggled with the pressure from the different groups within the same fellowship and these parallels do help us to understand more vividly the context in which the letter was written.

This then was the situation which Paul was addressing and out of which the Epistle comes. But what I have outlined is not always regarded as the best or the most orthodox understanding of the origins and meaning of the Epistle to the Romans. A different interpretation has grown up which has come to be accepted in large parts of the Church but this interpretation obscures the true origins of the letter and contains a number of false and, to say the least, unpauline assumptions. The true word of the Epistle to the Romans has been covered over and lost behind centuries of false interpretation. It is only in more recent years, thanks to the work of a number of scholars, especially E. P. Sanders, that we can rediscover the hidden word which Paul uttered at the time and see if that word has anything to say to our own generation.

This alternative interpretation of Paul's thinking stems, at least in part, from the Protestant Reformation and the writing of Martin Luther. Luther's views have been reinforced by much post-Enlightenment thinking, by the growth of introspection in western Protestantism and the growth in personal psychology. But the original fault lies with Luther. Luther was a monk who attacked the Church of his day for allegedly replacing the good news of God's forgiveness with a system of attaining pardon. He was a child of the late Middle Ages who lived his life within the perspective of a highly developed system of penance and indulgence. During this period self-examination had reached an unheard-of level of intensity. In order to cope with this the Church invented rules and a carefully regulated system of self-examination. Luther felt himself to be caught within that system and unable to climb out of it. In his struggles with his unforgiving conscience the Epistle to the Romans was an absolute Godsend. But unfortunately and perhaps inevitably he read the letter in the light of his own situation. When he read that we are justified by faith in Christ and not by works of the Law (Romans 5–8) he immediately identified the works of the Law with the penitential system which oppressed him. He felt he was some-body who constantly failed to lead the religious life success-fully and here was the answer. It was not the system which justified but faith in Christ! He believed he had found the true source of Christian freedom and began a religious – and also a political – revolution.

So began a tradition of interpreting Romans in which the centrality of the letter is found in chapters 5–8. Under this interpretation the human condition is seen as being utterly sinful and condemned to total futility. Human beings are unable to find a way out of their condition except by attempts to achieve their own justification with God. These human systems of achieving merit with a demanding God are them-selves futile and are equated with the Jewish Law, just as Luther equated the penitential system of his day with the Law. This tradition has been continued by the celebrated Lutheran theologian, Rudolf Bultmann. Bultmann saw the existential condition of humankind as being bound by the need to achieve the demands of a just God. Unfortunately, much of this interpretation has become part of the official formulas of our churches as well as our preaching of the Gospel. In the twentieth century such teaching has assumed a secularised form in association with a vulgarised psychology. Humankind is said to be bound by dark interior forces, unable to set itself free and so locked into tragedy from the outset. But whatever its origins, the popular view, both inside and outside the churches, is that Paul was the early Christian thinker who turned off the bright light of Jesus' teaching. He

was the one who condemned us all to original sin and guilt.
Christians are those who slough off this personal guilt by
means of their 'faith', a faith which when offered to God
guarantees salvation.

The great difficulty with this is that Paul never said any
such thing. We have read into Paul things which we think he
says and things which we think ought to be there. Unfortunately we have not spent enough time listening to what he
actually said. We have listened to what is going on in our
heads and in society round about us but not to what is
actually in the text. Once again the word has been hidden
from us by the noise of our society. The principal reason why
we have misunderstood Romans is because we have failed to
place it in its context. We have seen the letter as a theological
document containing generalised statements about the human
condition which are applicable to all people at all times,
rather than seeing it as a particular letter trying to answer a
particular ecclesiastical situation. It is actually just that – a
contribution to the debate between different Christians in
Rome in the middle of the first century CE about what God
is up to now if Gentiles can come into fellowship with him
without the necessity of accepting the whole of the Law. If
we take it out of that context then we actually lose the chance
to hear the word that God is speaking to us now because we
have removed the context in which that word was originally
spoken. It also risks allowing Paul's thought to be captive to
the fashions of each age rather than deriving its power from
the particularity in which it was spoken. A general word
about general things is much more easily subverted to the
patterns of the day than a particular word about particular
things.

The net result is that Paul's thought has been overlaid by
a gross anti-Judaism and a grossly negative understanding of
humankind, none of which is present in the Epistle to the
Romans itself. Now, however, we are able to free Paul from
these misconceptions and to release the word which his work
contains. We are also able to show how so much of the anti-
Judaism which has permeated European Christianity and
which has been said to be derived from his work is nothing

more, nor less, than a racism which has no place within any community of faith in the one God. We are also able to see that much of the negativity about human nature and the creation for which Christianity is said to be responsible is nothing to do with the Pauline texts. The hidden word can now be set free.

But what is this hidden word? What was it that Paul was trying to say? In order to find out let's look at one or two different passages in the Epistle and try to discover what Paul meant by them. Then, but only then, we will be able to return to the question of whether, once we have peeled away the layers of interpretation which obscure Paul's original meaning, there is anything left which can be of importance for us now.

Let's have a look, for example, at the passages in the early chapters of Romans where Paul appears to condemn all human beings as intrinsically sinful. The important passage is Romans 1:18–3:31. Chapter 3 verses 20–31 summarises the preceding verses and then leads through to the next stage of the Epistle but is an intrinsic part of this whole section. In accord with the advice given in previous chapters of this book let's read it through several times slowly and let its content sink into our consciousness . . .

The letter opens with greetings, thanksgivings and Paul's declaration that he will, at long last, be coming to visit the church in Rome. The reason is (1:14) that he is under an obligation to proclaim the Gospel to the Gentiles. Then (1:18ff) he moves into a description of the corruption of the pagan world which ends (3:9ff) with statements that no one is just and that all have sinned and fallen short of the glory of God.

These verses have led so many preachers and commentators into the simple view that Paul shows how all of us are fallen and corrupt but can be saved by faith in Christ. But a little thought and careful reading will show that this is not exactly what he is saying. As we have seen, the letter begins by trying to answer the accusation that Paul's thinking results in lawlessness. This was the conclusion that some people had come to after hearing the Epistle to the Galatians. There Paul

had said, for example, as he argued for justification by faith,
'Now it is evident that no one is justified before God by the
law'.[3] Well, people said, if that is the case then do you actually
need to follow the Law at all? Is morality of any benefit?
Shall we not sin then, so that grace can abound? And, of
course, there were even those who took this position to its
logical conclusion and began to abandon the moral code. One
man began an affair with his mother-in-law. Such reactions,
however, played into the hands of Paul's opponents. They
claimed that he was going too far and was licensing immorality. All this talk of justification by faith might sound very
good, but in fact it simply allows people to do what they like.
You need the Law in order to preserve people's sense of what
is right and wrong.

Paul objects (and it is at this point in the argument that
the Epistle to the Romans begins) that the Law doesn't save
you from sin. Having the Law doesn't seem to prevent Jews
from sinning. Sin is something which affects everyone, whoever they are. And the whole gist of his argument through
these verses is quite simply that – *sin affects all races*. Having
the Law is no protection against wrongdoing. The facts show
otherwise. In the verse 'all have sinned and fall short of the
glory of God'[4] the emphasis is upon the word 'all' and not
upon the word 'sinned'. So Paul is trying to show that Jews
and Gentiles are on the same footing before God. He even
produces an old Jewish argument to make his point, namely,
it is not having the Law but doing it which characterises
those who are God's people (2:13). So Paul is not trying to
prove the absolutely sinful nature of every individual. He is
responding to those who maintain you can't do away with
the Law by saying that merely having the Law is in itself no
protection against sin.

Indeed he makes the very important point (2:24–5, 26–7)
that even those who do *not* have the Law sometimes manage
to observe it naturally. 'When Gentiles, who do not possess
the law, do instinctively what the law requires, these, though

---

[3]Galatians 3:11.
[4]Romans 3:23.

not having the law, are a law to themselves. They show that what the law requires is written on their hearts'.[5] Even reading that verse should be enough to show that Paul does not think that all human beings are, without exception, helplessly under the control of sin, but there are other verses, earlier in the passage, which lead to the same conclusion. In the first chapter (1:18–32) Paul talks about the degradation of pagan life. He describes what happens to people who are without faith in or respect for the living God. And he is quite fierce, '. . . God gave them up to a debased mind and to things that should not be done. They were filled with every kind of wickedness, evil, covetousness, malice. Full of envy, murder, strife, deceit, craftiness, they are gossips, slanderers, God-haters . . .'[6] But this is only the result. It is not the condition. It is how people end up who forget the divine image within them and engage in wrongdoing. They then become so embroiled in sin that they are unable to do anything else. In other words Paul is describing how people become what they are. He is not saying that people in their original condition are always totally captive to sin so that they can do no good deeds without grace. In fact he is not talking about human nature in those theological or philosophical terms at all. That is something which later theologians and philosophers, particularly during the Protestant Reformation hundreds of years later, felt it necessary to talk about. Paul is just telling you how people get themselves into the state they do. He is not trying to prove human depravity. As one contemporary commentator says, 'Paul's aim . . . is to show that both Jews and Gentiles are sinful, and under the power of sin, and need the rescue that Jesus Christ provides. Into the question of whether in some way every single human being must be regarded as helplessly sinful, Paul simply does not go. That was a later debate, not Paul's.'[7]

But it is not just Paul's understanding of sin which gets distorted when he is taken out of context, it is also what he

[5]Romans 2:14–15.
[6]Romans 1:28–30.
[7]Ziesler, op. cit., p. 100.

says about the Law. Let's read through those same verses
again (1:18–3:31), this time looking out for the word 'law' . . .

   Above all remember the context – the argument about who
is part of the people of God. If Gentiles are allowed to be
part of that people without accepting all of the demands of
the Law as traditionally required, what happens to that Law?
Is it of no use any more? Can we no longer be proud of it?
Paul begins to answer these questions in chapter 3 (vv. 21ff).
Here he says that boasting is excluded because justification
is by faith 'apart from works prescribed by the law' (3:28).
This is the point at which preachers and teachers stop reading
the text and begin to read from something in their own heads.
They say, 'Ah, yes, what this means is that the Jews thought
they could win God's favour by their piety and good deeds.
Keeping the Law was the way to salvation. Obeying the Law
brought merit before God and this merit would be recognised
at the judgement day when those who had acquired a store
of merit would be given a place with the blessed.' Judaism,
the preacher goes on, was a meritocratic religion with obedience to the Law as the standard for the awarding of salvation
by God at the judgement. This way of thinking, we are told,
was explicitly condemned by Paul and definitively replaced
by a religion of justification by faith 'alone'. Judaism thus
stands condemned. However right that legalistic system may
have been in the past it was no longer valid – a new covenant
was given in Jesus for those who followed the new way of
justification by faith.

   Now all of us have heard sermons of this kind. The trouble
with them is that they do not correspond to what Paul said.
They are much more the result of the tradition left in Christianity by Martin Luther. Luther made great play in his day
with the use of the word 'merit'. He likened the purchase of
indulgences – a part of the penitential system operative in his
day – to the acquisition of merit. He found an easy target in
the Church of the time because the sale of indulgences
financed the rebuilding of St Peter's in Rome. This, he said,
was building up treasure upon earth, but the true treasury of
merit was in heaven, in the death of Christ. And not only
Luther but preachers since have used these passages in

Romans to condemn any human way of behaving which seeks to rely upon the acquisition of merit as the way to God's (or anybody else's) heart and to equate that way of behaving, quite without warrant, with 'Old Testament religion'.

Once again the difficulty is that Paul did not say anything of the kind. It is now clear, since the research of E. P. Sanders, that Judaism both before and at the time of Paul did not have within it any notion of acquiring merit and presenting it before God at the judgement. There is some small evidence of it after 70 CE, but that is after Paul's day. It can be said that Jewish writers talk about merit, but this is merit which has its reward *within this life* – its reward is in terms of success and prosperity on earth because of good deeds done and Torah followed. And if we think about it there is nothing wrong with looking at things in this way. If God made us then he has put the way of his Law in our hearts and if we all follow that way then the world will work as it should and people will naturally become happy and successful. This would only become an obnoxious notion if the law which was being followed was itself a selfish and exclusive code. But this particular Law – the Jewish Torah – which we are created to follow contains provision for helping the poor and the needy and proclaims as central the love of God and of one's neighbour as oneself. All of this and more can be found by a quick perusal of the Book of Leviticus and by reading what Jesus of Nazareth, a teacher of this Law, said. But the point is that it is a slander against Judaism, either then or now, to say that Judaism has as a central notion the idea of merit as something which will please God and so release from him his grace. As John Ziesler says in his commentary on Romans, 'In the Jewish literature contemporary with or earlier than the NT, salvation is *by God's grace* in election and covenant.'[8] Certainly Jews are expected to obey the Law but this is a *response* to God's beneficence in giving them the covenant, and not a prerequisite of any kind for his kindness.

If we think about it carefully it is quite simply monstrous to think otherwise. Any careful reading of the Psalms and of

[8]Ziesler, op. cit., p. 43.

the Hebrew Scriptures will show even the most casual reader that the Law is not regarded there as some sort of monstrous body of legalistic demands. It is a gift, God's gracious gift to the people, one which is sweet to the taste, and which once followed brings release and happiness. Psalm 119 is the obvious example of this. Here the psalmist delights in the Law of the Lord and hastens to follow its precepts.

> Lead me in the path of your commandments,
>   for I delight in it.

> I shall walk at liberty,
>   for I have sought your precepts.

> I find my delight in your commandments,
>   because I love them.[9]

And in the Book of Leviticus it is clear that the Law is a law which embodies grace, being concerned that the Israelite should be aware of the needs of the stranger in the land and should not lend money on interest and so on. The reason for this is not simply that God demands it but because the Israelites themselves were once strangers, aliens in Egypt, and were brought out by God's right hand. In other words obedience to the Torah is always a response and cannot affect God's grace because God's grace is given constantly – the Torah itself being the supreme example of it.

Of course none of this means that the idea of storing up merit as a way of obtaining God's grace does not affect religious people, whether they be Jews or Christians. It does affect them, but it is neither a Jewish nor a Christian notion because it implies that God can be manipulated. Certainly some religious people hold to it even though it is, as we shall see, quite opposed to the way of justification by faith which Paul teaches. But the point I am strenuously trying to make is that this is not a way of thinking about God which can be laid at the door of Judaism in St Paul's day or really in any day.

There is a further point about Paul's understanding of the

---

[9]Psalm 119:35, 45, 47.

Law which we should note. When he attacks obedience to the Law he does not do so because obedience to the Law leads to self-righteousness. It may or may not do that. Paul is against law-obedience because if salvation is through Christ then that is the end of the matter. He simply cannot or does not wish to talk about any other way of being saved. It is as if the light of Christ shines so brightly for him that everything else pales into total insignificance. It is not that he is deliberately negative about the Law, rather it is that he is extremely positive about salvation through faith in Christ. Moreover, law-obedience – although perfectly legitimate as such – can mean that people will erect artificial barriers between themselves and others which do not really matter. Paul believed that God accepted Jews and Gentiles equally. So when he talks about not boasting in the Law (3:28), he simply means that those who are Jewish Christians had no right to claim that their way of coming to God was ethically superior to that of Gentile Christians. It was not a superior way, it was simply a different way. From Paul's point of view *the ethical result was the same by means of justification by faith as it was by means of the Law*. Each way of coming to God brought the same behavioural results, in spite of what some people were saying. There was no evidence that having the Law made any difference in terms of human capacity for godly behaviour. So there was nothing to boast about. In either case nothing, whether law-obedience or justification, could affect God's covenantal grace. That was the same for all. God is not manipulated. God gives of himself.

The thing that many Christians find difficult to understand is that in his letters, and in Romans more than anywhere else, Paul does not reject the following of the Law as a rule of life. If anything, in the Epistle to the Romans, he strengthens his statements of that fact. Observance of the Law is what God intends of God's children. In chapter 7 he distinguishes between the Law and sin, saying that the Law is holy and good. He even argues in chapters 9–11 that the Law as a way of life has a continuing validity for all Christians. But this validity is redefined because he does actually ride roughshod over a number of the individual laws, particularly those about food, and he certainly ignores completely the traditional requirement of circumcision. In other words he does look at the Law in a new way, looking at it in the light of being righteoused by faith in Christ. That light shines stronger than the light of the Law alone because Paul believes that through faith in Christ Gentiles will find the essence of what the Law always stood for. But the Law is not disregarded as a means of understanding the ethical response which faith in God through Christ requires and, above all, the Law is not seen as a system of behaviour which brings merit upon the follower.

And so here is another point at which the word has been hidden by our own preoccupations. Our introspective concern with our own need for reassurance and merit – what Krister Stendhal, the great Swedish exponent of Paul, calls the introspective conscience of the West – has caused us to stumble. We have misinterpreted Paul by seeing in his work a condemnation of a merit-based system which did not actually exist. We have read our own needs into his work and as a result have led ourselves into a great deal of trouble, especially when we have assumed that Judaism was based upon such a merit-based 'legalistic' system. This has led us to condemn Judaism out of hand – something which Paul does not do. What he was trying to do was to find a way of allowing Jewish and Gentile Christians to live with one another. He was trying to show the Jewish Christians that the inner meaning of their faith was to be found in justification and the Gentile Christians that the ethical results of justification were the same as following the Law. He was also trying to persuade Gentile Christians that the Law had a good purpose in that it revealed the necessity for justification by faith. In this way he hoped the two groups would understand each other better and live together in a single fellowship.

But if that is the case one question still remains. What was it that Paul really meant by justification by faith? What was at the heart of his faith? We might well be able to see that he was not condemning human beings as innately corrupt. We might well be able to see that he was not confusing Judaism with merit-based religion. We might even be able to see that he was trying to find a way of allowing both Jew and Gentile to live together in the same fellowship. We might well have followed all that and be quite happy with it, but we will still want to ask – and this brings us back to the question of how the Epistle to the Romans applies to us now – what it was that forced him to say salvation was by justification by faith. What was it that pushed him into all this controversy, all this conflict? What was it that gave him a life's work of danger and controversy – controversy which still resonates with us now nearly two thousand years later? Obviously it was his own faith in Christ, yes. Obviously, also, he actually saw new Gentile Christians coming to faith in Christ and could not oppose the working of the Spirit. But there was something very powerful at work in Paul. What was it? When we have understood the context of the letter and removed all of the misunderstandings which have sprung up over the years, what was it that inspired Paul and tells us how he understood salvation? What is the hidden word?

To answer this let us go back to the text of the letter. First of all read through again the verses at the end of chapter 3, namely verses 9–31. Then let's turn to chapter 5 and read what Paul says there about justification. Read slowly and carefully the section which deals with justification from 5:1–6:11. Then read chapter 8, ending with the glorious passage which has been of so much hope and comfort to so many people through the centuries which begins, 'There is therefore now no condemnation for those who are in Christ Jesus.' It ends,

> For I am convinced that neither death, nor life, nor angels, nor rulers, nor things present, nor things to come, nor powers, nor height, nor depth, nor anything else in all creation, will be able to separate us from the love of God in Christ Jesus our Lord.[10]

Read these passages through carefully and slowly. Read them again, aloud to yourself if you can, and then let the words sink into your consciousness and become part of you.

[10] Romans 8:38–9.

Spend a day or so with these words, letting them come back into your consciousness every now and again, whenever you have a break in your working day. Let them become part of you for a while before you ask yourself what they essentially *mean*.

The reason for this is contained in their meaning. Paul was convinced that in the end God had set aside the effects of sin and that the believer was part of the life of God. Certainly sin matters and normally human beings are under the power or the occupation of sin, but Paul has also come to believe that God freely and actively puts people into a new relationship with himself. He transfers them from the kingdom of this world into the kingdom of his Son. The point is that human beings do not have to do anything to make him to do this. It is in his nature from the beginning to do it. In that new relationship the effects of sin are annulled and made void. A new creation comes about. This is essentially the same as the covenantal relationship which God has established with his people the Jews and it brings those who accept it into the same relationship with God that the Jews have always enjoyed. On the human side faith is the *response* of the person to this righteous (or 'righteousing') activity of God, not the cause of that activity. The essence of God's nature is to be gracious. The true nature of humankind is to have faith in that generosity and to respond to it.

The death of Christ on the cross is the place where that generosity is discovered. Here we find out what God is really like after all. In chapter 6 Paul makes it clear that the cross is not just the place where Jesus died, it is not just a point in history or an event in which the believer has to find some intellectual or moral significance. It is all of those things but it only has significance because it is an event in which the believer participates. Those who believe in Christ die with Christ to their sinful nature and are raised with him in the new life. He says,

> Do you not know that all of us who have been baptized into Christ Jesus were baptized into his death? Therefore we have been buried with him by baptism into death, so

that, just as Christ was raised from the dead by the glory of the Father, so we too might walk in newness of life. For if we have been united with him in a death like his, we will certainly be united with him in a resurrection like his.[11]

So for Paul justification is essentially something which happens to the believer, the one who dies and rises again with Christ. What happens is that the believer is transformed, he or she participates in the righteousness of God and his or her nature becomes part of the spiritual body of the Church. He or she is incorporated into Christ. Righteousness is not just reckoned to be there in spite of our sinful selves but actually *is* there because God is generous and gracious and has set aside the power of sin for those who believe in him. Justification is something which happens to the believer. Normally it does not happen because we are occupied by sin and pre-occupied by its power over our nature. Justification is God's hidden word to us and to all humankind. Our place is to see it at work in Christ's death and resurrection and by participative faith in those events actually to die to sin and live to life in Christ ourselves.

I have always felt that these words about justification are not easy for contemporary people to understand and so I was pleased, some years ago, to come across an image which enabled me to see just how all this talk in Paul's letters about justification might be translated into the speech of our day. I hasten to add that it is not my metaphor but rather my adaptation of a metaphor first used, as far as I know, by Bishop John Robinson in his excellent little book, *Wrestling with Romans*. The idea that sin occupies us gave Robinson the idea of comparing the human person to an occupied country, a country like France or Belgium during the war. Now there are several characteristics about life in an occupied country. One is that the country *is* occupied. By this I mean that the occupation is severe and fierce, the presence of the enemy is oppressive and almost inescapable. It pervades every aspect of life and no one can avoid its power over them. To a greater

[11]Romans 6:3–5.

or lesser extent all succumb to it. As we have seen, this is precisely Paul's view of sin. But it is also true that this is an *occupation*. The country is not ultimately that of the enemy. It is not the enemy's native land. The enemy comes from elsewhere. Apart from the occupation the country is a good and gracious place. It did not begin life occupied and should not in principle end life as an occupied territory. It was not made for this. This too is Paul's view of humankind. He speaks of the way in which the Gentiles have the possibility of observing the Law naturally. They are naturally good and gracious people.

In this occupation there are different forces at work. Some simply accept the situation as inevitable and collaborate with the occupying power. These are those Paul would say were living 'according to the flesh'. Others resist and fight on against the powers that oppress them. These live 'on the level of the spirit'. All are anguished and wish that it were otherwise, finding goodness almost impossible to practise in the situation. They cry out in their worst moments – almost anything we do is subverted, the good that we would do we cannot do!

Yet for those who are on the look-out there is an alternative. A new country is being born. There are resistance forces fighting away secretly who believe in a new life, a new dawn to things. This new dawn has already arrived for those who would have faith and act upon it. For these people nothing can separate them from the love of God and victory is already theirs. These freedom fighters are those who have become convinced that the captivity of the enemy is not the final truth and that God is already victorious over the enemy. The dawn of freedom is already present for those who would have faith.

In the celebrated and ridiculous television version of occupied France called *'Allo, 'Allo*, all of these elements are comically present and illustrate the main themes of Paul's theology. René, the bar owner, could be likened to a puzzled member of the church who cannot make up his mind which way he should turn. Should he collaborate with the enemy or belong to the Resistance? Should he tough it out by being as good as he can be in the circumstances following traditional ways, or should he succumb to the temptation to collaborate? Should he listen to the Resistance fighter with the beret and the turned-up collar who comes in at awkward moments and says, 'Listen, I will only tell you once . . .'?

In occupied France there were those who simply continued to be French, believing that something would happen in the end and that one day, somewhere in the future, liberation would come about. But there were also those who decided to do something about it and joined the Resistance. The woman Resistance worker in the television version of occupied France who says, 'I will only tell you once . . .' represents those who have taken the risk. They have placed their confidence in the actual presence of the new dawn and are now being righteoused by faith. She believes that God is at work bringing to nothing the effects of the occupying power and has decided to place her faith in the new life which is actually at work in her mortal body.

Obviously this analogy cannot be exact, and it is somewhat silly, but its very silliness might help us to understand one or two things about Paul's thinking. Firstly sin is extremely powerful, but it is not ultimate. Secondly, there is a new creation for those who would place their faith in Christ. This is not just a matter of acting as if God has set aside the effects of sin, but involves living in the reality of that transformation and co-operating with the work of God's transforming Spirit within.

Paul's message in Romans therefore is essentially an announcement of a reality that is hidden from us. The power of sin has blinded us to its real presence. But reflection on the death of Christ will enable us to see what God has done and is doing and then the word which he has spoken for us in Christ will be made clear. Then the powers of this world – the occupying forces of sin – will be broken in us and we will be set free.

In conclusion it is essential to remember that above all else Romans is an ecumenical work, trying to enable different sections of the Christian community in Rome to live together in mutual acceptance of each other. That was its initial purpose. What Paul says in the course of the Epistle about sin and salvation illustrates the answer to the initial ecumenical issue. In that sense Paul is an ecclesiastical politician first and foremost who does theology on the hoof, inventing it as he goes along in his desire to find theological support for what he wants to say about something else. He knows that God is bringing in the Gentiles to the faith of Israel, he can see it happening and acceptance of that reality is, he believes, essential for the health of the whole body.

Nor should we lose sight of the relevance of what he says for our own day. The Church today desperately needs to hear what he is saying about how different types of Christians ought to be able to live together, trusting that God is at work in them all in some hidden way. The message is as relevant today as it was then. But there is also something for us here in his understanding of sin and salvation. Human beings are occupied, not depraved. They can, through faith in Christ, actually participate in the new creation which he brings and be transformed into that reality. We have to learn to trust the workings, the hidden workings, of grace within us. It is there, and we have to listen and act.

I will only tell you once!

9

Magic Moments
(The Gospel of Luke)

Have you noticed how Luke does not seem to be very good at geography? If not, have a look at the way he describes Jesus' journey to Jerusalem. This journey begins towards the end of chapter 9 when '. . . he set his face to go to Jerusalem.'[1] In chapter 13 he is still on his way, for verse 22 records that 'Jesus went through one town and village after another, teaching as he made his way to Jerusalem.' He is warned that Herod is out to catch him but reaffirms his intention to go on to the city which murders the prophets. But then, in chapter 17, four chapters later, he is still on the journey and still only as far as the borderlands of Samaria and Galilee. Not really very far since chapter 9! But then, in chapter 18, we might begin to think he has got somewhere, for he takes the twelve aside and tells them, 'See, we are going up to Jerusalem, and everything that is written about the Son of Man by the prophets will be accomplished.'[2]

By this time we might have guessed that the actual geography of Palestine does not interest Luke very much. He is not recounting an actual journey, for if he were he would have managed to get Jesus and his party to their destination a lot quicker. He is using the motif of the journey to tell us something else. He is telling us that 'Jesus ascended to Jerusalem.' Indeed, there are several points in the narrative where that phrase, or something like it, is repeated and so becomes a leitmotif. In chapter 9, during the account of the

[1] Luke 9:51.
[2] Luke 18:31.

transfiguration, Luke tells of Moses and Elijah who 'appeared in glory and were speaking of his departure, which he was about to accomplish at Jerusalem.'[3] Then, in chapter 9 verse 51, we are told, 'When the days drew near for him to be taken up, he set his face to go to Jerusalem . . .' Then again, when he reaches Jerusalem in chapter 18 he tells the disciples that the time has come and that they are to go up to the city; then, in chapter 19 verse 28, we read, 'After he had said this, he went ahead, going up to Jerusalem', and then the drama of the test of his spirit unfolds.

After the crucifixion this Jerusalem leitmotif does not disappear. The risen Jesus appears to two of his followers on the Emmaus road, reminding them that the suffering predicted for the Christ by the prophets had to take place. Then when those two startled disciples *return* to the city, Jesus appears to all of them and among other things says, '. . . repentance and forgiveness of sins is to be proclaimed in his name to all nations, beginning from Jerusalem.' He continues, '. . . so stay here in the city until you have been clothed with power from on high.'[4] And as if to confirm this, when Luke begins the Acts of the Apostles he picks up the narrative from exactly this point, saying that Jesus had told the disciples to remain in Jerusalem until the Holy Spirit came upon them, '. . . and you will be my witnesses in Jerusalem, in all Judea and Samaria, and to the ends of the earth.'[5]

So Jerusalem is the pivotal point in the narratives, the place to which everything leads and from which everything proceeds. This place is the crux place, the fore-ordained point for the events of the crucifixion and resurrection of Jesus. This is when we have to remember that Luke is not writing history as we would understand it. He is not making a film of events as they happened. The Gospels are not old pathe newsreels. Luke, like the other evangelists, is interpreting what happened to Jesus and the disciples through the lens of his own mind and heart and giving his readers a metaphor

[3]Luke 9:31.
[4]Luke 24:47–9.
[5]Acts 1:8.

through which they in their turn can understand the events of the past. His metaphor is '*Jesus' death in Jerusalem is the fulcrum of history*'. He is saying that if you want to understand the events of Jesus' ministry you have to see them as central to God's plan in history. His death and resurrection, together with the outpouring of the Spirit, are the crucial events at the turning-point of time. All of the past history of the people of God leads up to that point, in Jerusalem, and all of the history of the Church since leads away from that point. Whoever you are, you are part of that grand plan and you have to see yourself as an actor within it if you want to understand what God is doing.

And so all of the players in Luke's Gospel and in the Acts of Apostles are people who are either going towards or coming away from that turning-point in history: the death and resurrection of Jesus of Nazareth in Jerusalem. They are all either on the journey up to Jerusalem, the city where the prophets predicted that the Messiah would suffer and die; or on the journey, armed with the power of the Spirit, away from Jerusalem out to the uttermost parts of the earth. The disciples are often shown as walking up to Jerusalem feeling puzzled and unknowing as if they are being led by forces greater than themselves. In Acts the same is true in reverse, they are blown out from this cataclysmic event by the wind of the Spirit. The Emmaus road story is a touching vignette of two of the disciples who were, as it were, walking out on it all, but who meet the risen Lord and are sent running back into the centre of the explosion to be caught up in the events.

Let us look at this grand design a little more closely by concentrating on one part of the narrative in Luke's Gospel – the point where Jesus deliberately involves the disciples in the divine plan. This is to be found in the section beginning at chapter 9 verse 1 and going on through until chapter 10 verse 24. Once again, following the method we have used so far in this book, read the passage through carefully and slowly several times. Spend some time with it. If possible read it aloud to yourself. In any case use your imagination to take it into yourself, become part of what it tries to say . . .

Chapter 9 of Luke's Gospel is the point where the whole

narrative changes gear. Up until that point there have been three main sections. The first (chapters 1–2) deals with the birth of Jesus the Messiah. The second (3:1–4:13) deals with his own personal discovery and appropriation of this identity in the baptism and outpouring of the Holy Spirit. This newfound vocation is tested in the wilderness. Then, at verse 14, Jesus returns to Galilee, 'filled with the power of the Spirit', to begin his ministry. He immediately goes to Nazareth, where he was brought up, and speaks in the synagogue on the sabbath. He announces his ministry there in unambiguous terms.

> The Spirit of the Lord is upon me,
> because he has anointed me
> to bring good news to the poor.
> He has sent me to proclaim release to the captives
> . . . to proclaim the year of the Lord's favor.[6]

This messianic announcement refers back to the jubilee year in which all debts were cancelled and all land reverted to its true owners, all contracts were ended and life began again from scratch. It also refers forward to the reign of the Messiah. This state of affairs, says Jesus, is available now and he is its minister.

Once Jesus has come to this point Luke begins the long section, which ends at the beginning of chapter 9, in which Jesus pursues this ministry in Galilee, making real what he had proclaimed in words in the synagogue. Luke portrays Jesus as proclaiming the good news and summoning disciples, healing the sick and raising the dead. The ministry at this stage is his. He does not commission the disciples, they are simply called and follow. But it is plain the ministry derives from his identity as the 'Holy One of God'. Then, in chapter 9, the whole tone changes. Jesus calls the twelve together and gives them the authority which, up until that point, had rested with him. We read, 'Then Jesus called the Twelve together and gave them power and authority over all demons and to cure diseases, and he sent them out to proclaim the kingdom

[6]Luke 4:18–19.

of God and to heal.'[7] What had been given to him during the baptism by John and what Jesus proclaimed as *his* ministry in his sermon in the synagogue at Nazareth, is now, in almost identical words, given to the disciples. They, in their turn, set out just as Jesus had set out after his appearance in his home town.

When they return (9:10), a number of singular events take place. These are not events of the same quality as the events which have occurred in the narrative up until now. They are not incidents on the way so much as peculiar happenings, events of a clearly special, almost transcendental nature. First, there is the feeding of the five thousand which, since it includes those actions which will be repeated at the Last Supper – 'he looked up to heaven and *blessed* and *broke* them, and *gave* them to the disciples . . .' – has an obvious eucharistic significance. This is followed by Jesus questioning his disciples about his identity: 'Who do the crowds say that I am?' When he asks them who *they* say he is, Peter answers, 'The Messiah of God'. At this Jesus predicts his suffering and death and speaks of how the cross is to be shared by those who would follow him. Then follows another disclosure situation, this time when Jesus is transfigured while praying, '. . . and his clothes became dazzling white.' Peter, James and John are weighed down with sleep during this event but they are awake enough to recognise who he is, just as Peter had recognised him when asked about his identity. The text emphasises this by saying, '. . . they saw his glory . . .' Then Jesus and the three come down from the mountain, the epileptic boy is cured, Jesus once again predicts that the Son of Man is going to be given up to the power of men, and then, almost immediately after that, '. . . he set his face to go to Jerusalem.'

So you can perhaps see that chapter 9 is a crucial chapter. It contains a cluster of happenings which all focus around the question of the recognition by the disciples of who Jesus really was and the commissioning of the disciples to share in that identity and activity themselves. Within the space of a

---

[7]Luke 9:1.

few short pages the disciples are called together and com-
missioned in the same terms that Jesus himself was com-
missioned in his baptism; there is a eucharistic feeding and
then two particular moments of recognition when first Peter,
and then Peter, James and John together are allowed to 'see
his glory'. All of these moments are accompanied by warnings
of suffering. Then, after all these rather extraordinary events,
Jesus suddenly sets his face to go to Jerusalem.

You might characterise the motifs or themes in the chapters
as *recognition, feeding, commissioning* and *action*. Central, however, is the *recognition*, for all of the others seem to depend
upon or flow from that. The moments of recognition are
surrounded by feeding and commissioning and lead to action.
This is what Luke really wants to write about and this
becomes clear once we realise that from the beginning of the
Gospel his interest in the actual geography or the actual
sequence of events is limited, overshadowed by his concern
to unearth the true pattern of what was going on in these
happenings. This pattern of recognition, feeding, commissioning and action is repeated at intervals in Luke's writings at
a number of crucial points in the narrative. This repetition
shows that he feels that there is, somehow, a basic pattern to
the way God deals with things and to the way in which we
respond to that. This is how people become part of the divine
plan in history and are caught up into God's activity in
history. Peter's recognition of Jesus as 'God's Messiah', and
the events which surround and stem from that recognition,
represent what he feels to be a basic movement or patterning
within the Gospel which demonstrates what God is really
doing with us and with the history of which we are a part.

We can see this pattern again if we look at chapter 10 of
the Gospel, at the events which take place as soon as Jesus
has set his face to go to Jerusalem. The sequence begins at
the end of chapter 9 with the incidents involving the men
who claim that they will follow Jesus wherever he goes
(9:57–62). They are turned away because they have not seen
how following involves the acceptance of loss. But if two are
turned away then immediately seventy-two are com-
missioned, a commissioning which is expressed in very similar

terms to those which Jesus used to commission the twelve a chapter earlier. They then return jubilant and Jesus is clearly moved. He says, 'See, I have given you authority . . .'[8] and thanks God that what was hidden from the wise is now revealed to the simple. Jesus himself clearly sees in their success proof of his identity. The truth is now out and they, as well as himself, have seen it. They now can take on the work which he felt was his alone. He turns to his disciples, saying, 'Happy the eyes that see what you are seeing . . . !' So the same pattern of *recognition* – nicely thrown into relief by the lack of recognition by the two single men of what was going on – *commissioning* and *action* is repeated, this time with a larger group of disciples. Starting from Peter's single act of recognition at the kernel of chapter 9 the commission is extended, first to include James and John, then the seventy-two.

At the end of the Gospel, in the face of the actual, but long-predicted suffering and death of Jesus, the whole process is repeated on a grand scale. This time it begins with the women at the tomb, extends to the two disciples at Emmaus, goes on through the eleven and then out to 'all the nations' (24:47). Let's look now at this part of the Gospel and see how Luke reveals what he feels to be the basic pattern of human response to the activity of God in Jesus during these last few chapters of his Gospel.

First of all read through the last three chapters (22–24) of the Gospel slowly. These three chapters begin in Jerusalem at the approach of the Passover and end with the final commissioning of the disciples by the risen Christ and his parting from them at Bethany. These are the central events of the Lukan saga, so read them slowly several times, again aloud to yourself if you can, and let them be part of your inner life for a day or so. One little exercise in grasping their significance might be to note carefully all of the references to 'seeing'. There are a large number of them and they give much of the colour to the narrative.

Just before chapter 22 begins Jesus has warned the disciples

[8]Luke 10:19.

to be awake and watch out for the coming cataclysm. At the Passover supper (22:14) he warns them again that the end is approaching, singling out Simon Peter in particular. Then once again he deliberately invests them with the kingship which his Father vested in him and recalls their first commissioning, when he sent them out without purse or pack. He reminds them that then they lacked nothing, but warns them that now things will be different because allegiance to him will provoke others to violence against them. Their recognition of him will be put to the test. And throughout chapters 22 and 23 this is what happens. The sequence of events unrolls and is narrated so that we can see just who continues to recognise the Christ in a time of total crisis. There are some who recognise him and some who do not. At the crucial moment even Peter, the one who had recognised him first of all and who has protested his loyalty most fiercely, is tested and fails. This test is summed up in the reaction of the thieves who are crucified with him. One of them recognises who he is and is immediately received into the kingdom, but the other does not. The centurion is shown to be one who does recognise what was going on and 'he praised God'. Then the women, who during his ministry had supported him and loved him, are shown to be standing there watching and then, after the sabbath, they go to the tomb to embalm the body. They are the first to be given a moment of recognition, but then (as today) what the women saw is not believed.

Then all is summed up in the final chapter and the story of the Emmaus road. Whether or not this story is based in fact or not does not matter. What does matter is that it is a story which encapsulates everything that Luke has been trying to say about Jesus and our response to him as the revelation of God's divine plan. Here in miniature is what the Gospel has been saying through all of its twenty-four chapters. Here all of the themes are recapitulated and brought together in one tiny gem of a story. Here the basic pattern of Luke's thinking, a pattern which is the result of reflection upon the whole of Jesus' ministry and revealed in whole or in part at various crucial points in that ministry, is concentrated into one, single incident. What matters is not so much the historical truth of what happened – and something must have triggered it all off – as the psychological truth of the pattern of recognition and response that it reveals. This is how things are. It is through this pattern of unknowing, feeding, recognition and commissioning that they, and all of us, are drawn into the activity of the liberating God who was in Jesus.

Let's look at the story in more detail. First of all Jerusalem is the invisible pivot around which the story hangs. Emmaus is said to be about seven miles away from the city, the two discuss events which have taken place there and at the end return there in great haste. The story swivels around the city just as Luke's version of history swivels around it. Then there is the way in which the two talk about what has happened with Jesus present but do not know who he really is. This pattern is found throughout the first section of the Gospel itself up until chapter 9. In that first section, and indeed even after Peter's declaration and Jesus' commission, the disciples are with Jesus but do not give him the recognition that his true identity deserves. In that section the disciples ask him the meaning of things he has said (8:9). John's disciples ask if he is the one they should expect (7:19), but devils (8:28), Gentiles (7:2) and prostitutes (7:37) do recognise him. On the other hand the Pharisees are offended (5:21) and the disciples are puzzled (8:25). All of this is summed up in the simple image of two people walking with a stranger and not knowing who he is.

Then, in Jesus' question asking them what they are talking about and Cleopas' outburst in response, a whole world of longing and puzzlement is revealed. What Cleopas says contains all of the longing for salvation which lies behind the tentative loyalty of the disciples through the Gospel, their obvious desire for a new vision and clarity over the ways of God. It contains all of their longing and their stumbling. His words, 'But we had hoped that he was the one to redeem Israel . . .'[9] are full of all of the questions, all of the diseases, all of the desires which have been brought to Jesus throughout

[9]Luke 24:21.

the Gospel narrative. 'A man in the crowd said to him . . .', 'Someone asked him . . .', '. . . the tax gatherers and other bad characters were crowding in to listen to him . . .', 'A man of the ruling class put this question to him . . .' These searchings and longings go on throughout the Gospel in the most insistent way. They are summed up by the evident frustration in Peter's voice earlier in the narrative when he says to Jesus, 'Look, we have left our homes and followed you'.[10] All this is encapsulated in Cleopas' words. They had hoped for so much but now it all seems to have evaporated away.

Jesus' answer mirrors all of the answers which he had given to the disciples in the course of the Gospel, telling them parables, pointing things out to them, persuading, cajoling, warning, urging them to look at things this way rather than that. ' "Oh, how foolish you are, and how slow of heart to believe all that the prophets have declared! Was it not necessary that the Messiah should suffer these things and then enter into his glory?" '[11] This is precisely the attitude that Luke shows Jesus as demonstrating towards his followers earlier in the narrative – as someone who continually says, 'Don't you see . . .' But then at last comes the supreme moment of recognition when '. . . their eyes were opened and they recognised him'. Once again recognition of who Jesus was comes in a particular moment, and is a point at which all of the doubts and fears fall away and recognition and relief and joy flood the heart.

What is remarkable about the Emmaus road story is that it is a summary of all of the previous 'magic moments' of recognition found earlier in the Gospel. It is a story which concentrates in a few sentences what the Gospel narrative has taken so long to say in the chapters before it. In particular, it contains all of the motifs, all of the themes which are present in the events of chapter 9. As we saw, in that chapter Peter recognises the Lord. This moment of recognition is placed by Luke within the context of a number of events which, when

[10]Luke 18:28.
[11]Luke 24:25.

seen together, form a pattern of happenings which is then found, like the theme of a symphony, in other parts of the Gospel. It is then repeated, in a particularly concentrated form, as a final coda to the whole, in this incident on the Emmaus road. In chapter 9 Peter's recognition of the true nature of Jesus is placed next to a eucharistic moment, a moment of epiphany on a mountain top and a commissioning. It is also accompanied by warnings from Jesus about the inevitability of suffering in this whole process. All of these motifs are present here too. The recognition of Jesus' identity takes place during the breaking of bread. It is a high moment of epiphany which comes to an abrupt end as he vanishes and they are left with ordinary existence once again, just as the moment of transfiguration left Peter, James and John with the disciples and the petulant father at the foot of the mountain. But just as the disciples find themselves in mission earlier in the Gospel so here the recognition precipitates action as they run back to Jerusalem and tell the others. When they reach Jerusalem there is another appearance and the commission to preach the Gospel to all the nations. In and through all of this suffering is never forgotten. This time not because of any words of Jesus himself so much as the marks of the nails on his hands. So the pattern is once again repeated, *recognition, feeding, commissioning* and *action*, but all against a background of inevitable loss and suffering.

For Luke this is how things really were for those who came to a point of crisis. By means of this pattern they are brought into the divine movement in history and are converted to the way of the Messiah. This pattern continues to exercise its influence on his writing when we move into the Acts of the Apostles. It is as if there is a rush of holy wind from Jerusalem, from the crucified and risen Jesus, which carries the disciples out to the far ends of the earth. As the disciples are caught in this movement there are further moments when their eyes are opened to the unforeseen implications of what Jesus was for the world. Paul comes to his moment of recognition on the road to Damascus (Acts 9). Peter, too, is converted again, this time over the question of food offered to idols (Acts 10). Once again the narrative makes a great deal of the need to 'see' the truth and Paul has scales which fall away from his eyes when Ananias cures his blindness. As the story in Acts proceeds both Peter and Paul refer back to these magic moments as containing the source of their authority to do what they are doing and say what they are saying. These magic moments have liberated them and energised their lives. In chapter 26, speaking before Agrippa, Paul defends his work in terms of obedience to the heavenly vision and says that he is called to the Gentiles '. . . to open their eyes so that they may turn from darkness to light'.[12] At the very end of the narrative, in a closing eulogy, Paul speaks to the local Jewish leaders in the same terms, quoting Isaiah in defence of his mission to the Gentiles, 'For this people's heart has grown dull . . . and they have shut their eyes . . .'[13]

The inner, hidden meaning of Luke's writing is, then, his emphasis on recognition. Jesus came to enable those who were blind to see what was really the case – that God was bringing salvation to all those who turn to him, irrespective of their race or original faith. This happens when, in a moment of recognition, a magic moment, we turn and accept that the ministry of Jesus is the work of God. At that point a holy wind involves us in the hidden work of God in history, blowing from the death and resurrection of Jesus in Jerusalem, the pivotal point of history, into the future where all shall come into the kingdom – but first the blind, the lame, the women at the tomb, centurions, the poor and the children. They in their poverty and weakness are the first to see. The disciples were waverers. Others resist through hardness of heart. This magic moment is not, however, without its cost. The recognition is also a recognition that the suffering of Jesus does not belong to him alone. His followers will have to bear the cross as well. But that being the case the world is well lost.

In the chapel of my college the painting behind the altar depicts the supper at Emmaus. When I was a student I used to sit entranced by it during services, and have remembered

[12]Acts 26:18.
[13]Acts 28:27.

it more clearly than any of the sermons we heard. When I am back at the college for any reason I always try to find a moment to go into the chapel to absorb some of its magic once again. It is a modern painting by Ceri Richards and depicts the very moment when the disciples knew that it was Jesus. On the table there is bread broken and Jesus sits behind with hands uplifted and the nail marks clearly visible. The light through the half-open door forms a bright cross behind his body. The two disciples are half seated, half standing, pushing their chairs back as they fall away from the moment of truth, again lifting their hands in terror and joy. It is a very moving and powerful statement. Ceri Richards has caught in paint the very moment of truth as it was for Luke the evangelist, a moment which is hidden behind the words of his Gospel and which is hidden within human life all of the time. Our lives will only be more human and more godly when we come to encounter the same moment for ourselves.

Afterword

I was once part of a Bible Study group in Africa. My wife and I went because we felt the need to study the Bible together with other Christians and be sustained by what it said. It was an ecumenical group and had two or three religious sisters as members. I remember that we decided to read Isaiah 40–66 week by week. When it was my turn I looked up all of the commentaries and talked at length about the way in which these words were a prophecy of return from the exile in Babylon after the accession of Cyrus. I went into great detail about the particular servant passage I had been given and speculated as to who this might have been. Was the servant a particular figure of Israelite history? Was he the imprisoned King Jehoiachin? What could Christians make of all this? It was the sort of Bible study you might have expected from someone who was afraid of losing his intellectual credibility and was out, if not to impress others, at least to convince himself that he knew something about the text. I do not remember the reaction of the group.

What I do remember was my reaction when the two sisters came to lead the group on their section of the text. We heard little or nothing about the religious and political background. We certainly heard nothing about the questions of authorship or the author's intended meaning of the text. We simply read the text through slowly, with plenty of silence, and said what it meant for us now. I can remember my reaction. I was puzzled and not a little disturbed. I didn't want to study the Bible like this. This was Bible study, I thought, for intellectual softies.

I was proved wrong. Everybody there came away feeling

very moved and encouraged by what had gone on. Isaiah had been allowed to speak to us without encumbrance. Our exiled position as British expatriates working in a foreign country, looking for the salvation of God, had been highlighted and spoken to. We came away knowing that there was a highway in our desert for our God. None of the intellectual questions about the text had been entirely dropped. My queries had been politely and clearly answered by people who had read the commentaries. It was not an anti-intellectual presentation. The point is that I still remember it now, some fifteen years later. I remember the quiet voices of the sisters and the text itself coming to life beneath our eyes.

The symbolism of the text had been allowed to affirm itself. It was a text about exile and return. We had been allowed to enter into that pattern, or rather been taken into that pattern, and it had spoken its hidden word to us. It had been *true*, then and there for us, a group of exiles in a far country. The previous week's study had not been so successful because my need to intellectualise had interfered with the group's desire to struggle with the text and so *be made true*. I had also risked the wrath of a more fundamentalist member of the group, the chaplain of the school in which we were meeting, and the group had nearly degenerated into an argument between him and me. Both of us had been as bad as each other. But the quiet insistence of the sisters that there was another way of reading the text had cleared the air and we sat together, Anglican and Catholic, radical and fundamentalist, good and bad, clever and simple, under the same word and had found the word which our preoccupations had hidden from our eyes.

I have told this story because it illustrates in a clear and vivid way something of what this book has tried to say about how to read the Bible. The Bible is a book of which we are a part. Its great narrative and its inherent patterns are part of us and we part of them. We shall discover that the Bible is 'true' only when we allow ourselves to become part of that narrative and find the patterns of which it speaks buried deep within our psyches. That was true for us in the group when we suddenly knew that Second Isaiah, as well as speaking to the exiles in Babylon was also speaking to us. We became part of the word. We nearly were prevented from hearing that word because of our intellectual and theological preoccupations.

When asked whether the Bible is 'true', our response must be yes, a magnificent, affirmative yes. But this is not because it is literally true. The history related did not always happen as the text states. Nor is the Bible true because scholars have struggled with the language or the archeology and can now say that perhaps this small part is true. There are places where the text is historically accurate and places where it is not. The task of any reader is to know, as part of his or her quest for truth, why that is the case. What were the pressures which prevented the writer from allowing history to be represented accurately? Once that question is answered then the hidden patterns will be more readily available. The Bible is true because it contains these hidden patterns. It is true because it contains within it the truth about ourselves. If we live as if we are part of its narrative and as if its hidden patterns are life-giving then we shall live within the word which gives life. We shall live as we were meant to live.

This does not mean to say that we have to give up asking questions about the text. Just the contrary. We have to keep on looking at the text in the most rigorous way simply because rigorous enquiry is the only way in which the inner patterns which are actually present will be discovered and set free. If we simply accept the text uncritically then we risk reading out of the text no more than what we actually want. Then we abandon ourselves to patterns of living which are the product of our own imaginations or of the spirit of our own age. Intellectual enquiry is the safeguard we have against being subverted by fashion or sentimentality. We cannot rest content that we know all that is necessary simply because we have the text. The text is not its own interpreter.

Nor, on the other hand, are we our own interpreters. Simply explaining the origins of the text or inventing a neat theory about its authorship is only a partial explanation. The text is also a blessing. Human beings need the re-ordering power of God. The point is that our psyches become disordered. Our patterns of living become dislocated and confused. We need to have the inner patterns of our souls set to rights, put back in the shape in which they were created, re-ordered by the power of God found within the hidden patterns of Scripture. Think for a moment of the effect that listening to the story of Joseph or the Beatitudes being read aloud has upon us. People visibly unwind, settle back, open up their inner spirits and allow the words to settle within their souls as a healing grace. When that happens the Scriptures are true in a much more profound sense than the truth which is so often spoken of in religious circles.

When we read the Bible we are exploring our own selves. We are reading our own history, talking about our own struggle with God, our discovery of liberation. The truth of the Bible is not so much something which we accept or reject. Rather the truth of the Bible is something which is made as we struggle with its narrative and the patterns which are hidden within that narrative. Like Jacob's struggle with the angel we discover the truth of God as we struggle with his word and allow ourselves to hear, and to be questioned, but also to be blessed and shaped by the life which it bears.

Recommended Reading

GENERAL BOOKS

Two good general introductions are: James Fischer, *How to Read the Bible – A Basic Contemporary Guide For People of All Faiths* (Prentice Hall 1987, Crucible paperback 1988) and William H. Shannon, *Seeking the Face of God* (Collins/Fount 1988).

More advanced and extremely interesting: Frances Young, *The Art of Performance – Towards a Theology of Holy Scripture* (Darton, Longman and Todd 1990) and Nicholas Lash, 'Performing the Scriptures' in his collection of essays *Theology on the Way to Emmaus* (SCM Press 1986).

Of particular relevance to both the first section of this book and to individual chapters in the second section are: Jonathan Magonet, *A Rabbi's Bible* (SCM Press 1990) and John A. Sanford, *The Man Who Wrestled With God* (Revised Edition, Paulist Press 1987). This last book is exceptionally good.

Another book which appeared just as I was coming to the end of writing this book is: Robin Lane Fox, *The Unauthorised Version* (Viking 1991). This is very important but is only the beginning of wisdom. The review by Robert Alter in *The Times Literary Supplement* for 20 December 1991 should be cut out, pasted inside the front cover and referred to during reading.

DIFFERENT APPROACHES

A. There are a number of introductions to the spiritual life – probably too many! The approach followed here was developed by me in: Melvyn Matthews, *The Hidden Journey* (Fount 1989).

As far as the Bible is concerned: John Eaton, *The Contemplative Face of Old Testament Wisdom* (SCM Press 1989) is particularly useful.

In terms of a general understanding of spirituality not much can better: Ann and Barry Ulanov, *Primary Speech – A Psychology of Prayer* (SCM Press 1982).

B. On the Bible as literature and the theology of story the following are important:

Ed. Alter and Kermode, *The Literary Guide to the Bible* (Collins 1987).
Gabriel Josipovici, *The Book of God – A Response to the Bible* (Yale 1988).
Alastair MacIntyre, *After Virtue* (Duckworth 1981) – a dense but crucially important book for anybody concerned with the life of our times.
Trevor Dennis, *Lo and Behold! The Power of Old Testament Storytelling* (SPCK 1991).
William J. Bausch, *Storytelling, Imagination and Faith* (Twenty-third Publications, Connecticut 1988).
Joseph Campbell, *The Power of Myth* (Doubleday 1988). (I am indebted to the Revd Bob Delap for showing me this book.)

C. The Jungian implications are explored in a number of books, especially those by Sanford, whose study of Jacob, Joseph and Moses is cited above. Also important are:

Ann and Barry Ulanov, *Cinderella and Her Sisters* (Westminster Press 1983).
Gerald Slusser, *From Jung to Jesus – Myth and Consciousness in the New Testament* (John Knox Press 1986).
Brian Thorne, *Behold the Man – A Therapist's Meditations on the Passion of Christ* (Darton, Longman and Todd 1991).

D. There are a large number of books about Ignatian spirituality and its use of Scripture. The most accessible is, of course: Gerard W. Hughes sj, *God of Surprises* (DLT 1985). See also: Ed. Philip Sheldrake, *The Way of St Ignatius of Loyola* (SPCK 1991).

INTERPRETING THE BIBLICAL PASSAGES

The footnotes in each chapter should be referred to for specific books but the following are the most useful:

On Creation: Robert Faricy, *Wind and Sea Obey Him* (SCM Press 1982) and Jurgen Moltmann, *God in Creation* (SCM Press 1985).

On Joseph: Thomas Mann, *Joseph and His Brothers* (Penguin 1978).

On the Beatitudes: Simon Tugwell OP, *Reflections on the Beatitudes* (DLT 1980).

On the Epistle to the Romans: John Ziesler, *Paul's Letter to the Romans* (SCM Press 1991) and E. P. Sanders, *Paul* (Oxford Past Masters Series 1991).

On St Luke's Gospel: John Drury, *Tradition and Design in Luke's Gospel* (DLT 1976).

The Study Guide which accompanies this book – *Finding Your Story*, ed. Melvyn Matthews – contains a number of further references, particularly to the literature on the Scripture passages above.